THE SURPRISING
TRUTH
ABOUT
DEPRESSION

THE SURPRISING
TRUTH
ABOUT
DEPRESSION

Medical Breakthroughs
that Can Work for You

HERBERT WAGEMAKER, M.D.
with PETER DAMIAN BELLIS

ZondervanPublishingHouse
Grand Rapids, Michigan

A Division of HarperCollinsPublishers

The Surprising Truth about Depression
Copyright © 1994 by Herbert Wagemaker, M.D., with Peter Damian Bellis

Requests for information should be addressed to:
Zondervan Publishing House
Grand Rapids, Michigan 49530

Library of Congress Cataloging-in-Publication Data

Wagemaker, Herbert
    The surprising truth about depression : medical breakthroughs that
can work for you / Herbert Wagemaker, with Peter Damian Bellis.
    p. cm.
    Includes bibliographical references and index.
    ISBN 0-310-40101-1 (pbk.)
    1. Depression, Mental—Popular works. I. Bellis, Peter Damian.
I. Title.
RC537.W23   1994
616.85'27–dc20   93-37594
                                                                       CIP

Some of the names in this book have been changed to protect the privacy of the individuals described.

All Scripture quotations, unless otherwise noted, are taken from the HOLY BIBLE: NEW INTERNATIONAL VERSION®. Copyright © 1973, 1978, 1984 by International Bible Society. Used by permission of Zondervan Publishing House. All rights reserved.

Edited by Dan Runyon
Cover design by Mary Cantu
Cover photo copyright © Superstock, Inc.

Printed in the United States of America

94 95 96 97 98 99 / DH / 10 9 8 7 6 5 4 3 2 1

This book is dedicated to
four good friends and respected colleagues:

Henlee Barnette, Ph.D.
Robert Cade, M.D.
Wayne Oates, Ph.D.
Theodore VanPatten, M.D.

Contents

When the Problem Is Alcohol
What About Prescription Drugs?
Summing Up

PART THREE
When It Is Depression

Introduction:
A Message of Hope

About ten to twenty percent of us will become depressed or anxious at some point in our lives. Depression is a painful fact of life. Whenever we feel depressed or anxious, we think we should be able to pull ourselves up by the bootstraps and go on with life. "What's wrong with us?" we ask. "Why can't we snap out of it? Why do we feel so lousy?" When we can't "will" our pain away, we become upset and confused.

I think about my own periods of depression. I am a Christian, and Christians are not supposed to get depressed. (I know that's written down somewhere, not in so many words, but the meaning seems clear enough.) God meant for my life to be full of joy and happiness. Yet in spite of my faith in God's plan, I am sometimes depressed and unhappy. Why do I feel this way? The obvious answer to my misguided spiritual self is that somehow I have a spiritual problem. I must have some unconfessed sin buried deep within my past. Or maybe I'm not spending enough time with the Lord. Maybe I'm not acting as the witness I should be.

Another thought comes to my mind, an unwelcome thought, that I am the only Christian ever to suffer in this manner. I am the only Christian ever to be depressed! Surely none of my Christian friends feel the way I feel. What would they think if they knew? They would think I had some sort of a spiritual problem. And because I am absolutely sure of their unvoiced opinion, an opinion which carries with it the weight of truth because it is unvoiced, I add to the silence.

Now hold on a minute! Do I really believe that depression is caused by a black mark on my soul? Do I really believe that if you're depressed, you need to work through your pain? No, I do not. For too many years the Christian community has been told a lot of things about depression that are just not true. I know that depression is not usually caused by any spiritual deficiency. (Thank God for all that I learned in medical school.) I know that some people can be depressed and yet still be on the road to spiritual wholeness. And I know that other people can be free from the symptoms of depression and still lack spiritual commitment.

Depression Is Not a Dirty Word

For many Christians, depression is a dirty word. Those who suffer from this disease, and it is a disease, usually suffer in silence. They tell no one. Not husbands. Not wives. Not friends. No one. At least fifty percent of those suffering from depression never seek help. I think the percentage is even higher among Christians. Those Christians who do speak up do so only when they can bear the pain no longer. They are hesitant at first, and usually seek the advice of a pastor or family physician. They rarely seek the advice of a qualified psychiatrist, for such an act would be an open admission that they really are crazy. Besides, there aren't many psychiatrists who are also practicing Christians, though there are some.

I Am a Christian, and I Am Also a Psychiatrist

I was brought up in a Christian family and committed my life to Christ when I was in the fifth grade. I attended Hope College, but later graduated from Wheaton College, and after that I spent some time in seminary. Since I finished my psychiatric residence in 1971, I have worked in community mental health, taught at a university, run a state hospital, and conducted research in schizophrenia. I am now in private practice. I am a teacher, a psychiatrist, and a researcher, but above all, I am a Christian.

The good news I bring is that Christians do not need to suffer depression in silence. Depression is not caused by something spiritual, at least in most cases; it is caused by something physical, something biochemical. Depression is the result of a biochemical imbalance in the brain and so it can be treated through medication.

This book is for Christians who suffer from depression or depression-related illnesses in silence. Most of the case histories are taken from the lives of Christians, many who have been helped with medication as well as through counseling. Here is a book of hope, a book of good news. My message is simple. Depression can be diagnosed and treated. You don't have to suffer in silence alone. Depression is not a spiritual problem. You can be helped; you can live a normal life again. You can.

JUST WHAT IS A

CHRISTIAN!! ??

PART ONE

Diagnosis

— 1 —

Am I Depressed?

Everybody gets depressed from time to time. But how do you know if you're really depressed, or suffering from something else? How do you distinguish between normal grief, or what some call "the blues," and true depression? Perhaps the best way to answer this question is to begin by asking some more.

Problems with Sleeping

The first thing I ask of new patients is whether or not they are having trouble sleeping. People who are depressed always seem to have trouble sleeping. Some can't seem to get enough sleep, often lying in bed twelve, fourteen, even sixteen hours a day. For others the opposite is true. They may go to bed around ten or eleven, and yet they are still watching the clock at midnight, one, and even two. When they do fall asleep, they usually manage only a couple of hours before they wake up. Most have great difficulty falling asleep again. Some can't get back to sleep at all.

The next set of questions I need to ask are not so simple to answer. How well are you functioning? How are you getting on with your day-to-day life?

It's no big deal if you have a couple of sleepless nights. That happens to all of us. But when you're awake night after night, your ability to face life changes. You become irritable. You have a hard time relating to others, your wife, your husband, your kids, your peers. You begin to harbor feelings of hopelessness and helplessness. You simply don't have the energy or the desire to do much of anything. Even writing out a grocery list seems an impossible task.

The same is true if you're sleeping too much. A few days when you can't get out of bed does not mean you are depressed. But if your sleep-filled days become weeks, then you may have a problem. The bottom line either way, whether you're sleeping too much or not enough, is you don't have the energy to get on with your life. You feel exhausted, overwhelmed, sad, disinterested. You are depressed.

When patients complain of sleeping problems, I consider them depressed until proven otherwise. In my experience, sleeping problems are the best indication of depression. But there are a number of other symptoms that suggest depression as well.

Other Symptoms

We've all heard of the stereotypical housewife who eats chocolate when she's upset. But there is more than a grain of truth to this stereotype. If you are eating more than you used to, or if you have little or no appetite, you may also be depressed. The same is true if you are crying excessively, or for no reason, if you have been having feelings of panic, perhaps dizzy spells, if you find yourself becoming indecisive or confused, or if you just feel angry. If you are depressed, you may be suffering from any or all of these symptoms.

Lastly, you may be depressed even if your symptoms are only physical. Some of the more common physical symptoms are headaches, neck tension, constipation, vague abdominal pains, even aches and pains in the joints. Of course many people who

ZUNG DEPRESSIVE EVALUATION SCALE

	None or a little of the time	Some of the time	A good part of the time	Most of the time
1. I feel down-hearted and blue.	1	2	3	4
2. Morning is when I feel best.	4	3	2	1
3. I have crying spells or feel like crying.	1	2	3	4
4. I have trouble sleeping at night.	1	2	3	4
5. I eat as much as I used to.	4	3	2	1
6. I still enjoy sex.	4	3	2	1
7. I notice that I am losing weight.	1	2	3	4
8. I have trouble with constipation.	1	2	3	4
9. My heart beats faster than usual.	1	2	3	4
10. I get tired for no reason.	1	2	3	4
11. My mind is as clear as it used to be.	4	3	2	1
12. I find it easy to do the things I used to.	4	3	2	1
13. I am restless and can't keep still.	1	2	3	4
14. I feel hopeful about the future.	4	3	2	1
15. I am more irritable than usual.	1	2	3	4
16. I find it easy to make decisions.	4	3	2	1
17. I feel that I am needed and useful.	4	3	2	1
18. My life is pretty full.	4	3	2	1
19. I feel that others would be better off if I were dead.	1	2	3	4
20. I still enjoy the things I used to.	4	3	2	1

suffer from such physical problems are not depressed, but they may be a sign of hidden or masked depression, and they need to be addressed. I pay very close attention to my patients when they complain of physical problems.

The Zung Depressive Evaluation Scale

If you suspect you might be depressed, there are some pretty good self-rating scales that can give you some idea if you need to seek help. One is the Zung Depressive Evaluation Scale (see previous page).[1] This scale consists of twenty questions that address the general state of your emotional health. The answers range from none or some of the time to most of the time, and are given a score of one to four points. To determine whether you are depressed or not, add up the total points. A score of twenty to thirty points means that you are not depressed. A score of thirty-one to forty points means you suffer from some depression and may need help. A score of forty-one to eighty points means that you are moderately to severely depressed and need to seek help from a biological psychiatrist.

The Social Readjustment Rating Scale

Another scale used to determine the likelihood of your becoming depressed is the Social Readjustment Rating Scale (see next page).[2] The more stress you have in your life, the greater the possibility you will become depressed. This scale measures the amount of stress in your life by assigning a mean score to a variety of life events. The scope is limited to only those events which have occurred within the last year. The higher the score, the greater the stress level. Of course the conclusions to be drawn from any scale of this type are not definitive. What is important to one person is not necessarily important to another. But there are a number of events—the death of a loved one, changing jobs, getting married, getting divorced—which do have a profound effect on most people.

The scoring is as follows:

0–49   no life crisis
50–199   mild life crisis
200–299   moderate life crisis
300 or more major life crisis

SOCIAL READJUSTMENT RATING SCALE

Rank	Life Event	Mean
1.	Death of Spouse.	100
2.	Divorce.	73
3.	Marital separation.	65
4.	Jail term.	63
5.	Death of close family member.	53
6.	Personal injury or illness.	53
7.	Marriage.	50
8.	Fired at work.	47
9.	Marital reconciliation.	45
10.	Retirement.	45
11.	Change in health of family member.	44
12.	Pregnancy.	40
13.	Sex difficulties.	39
14.	Gain of a new family member.	39
15.	Business readjustment.	39
16.	Change in financial state.	38
17.	Death of a close friend.	37
18.	Change to a new line of work.	36
19.	Change in number of arguments with spouse.	35
20.	Mortgage over $10,000.	31
21.	Foreclosure of mortgage or loan.	30
22.	Change in responsibilities at work.	29
23.	Son or daughter leaving home.	29
24.	Trouble with in-laws.	29
25.	Outstanding personal achievement.	28

26. Spouse begins or stops work.   26
27. Begin or end school.   26
28. Change in living conditions.   25
29. Revision of personal habits.   24
30. Trouble with boss.   23
31. Change in hours/conditions.   20
32. Change in residence.   20
33. Change in schools.   20
34. Change in recreation.   20
35. Change in church activities.   19
36. Change in social activities.   18
37. Mortgage or loan less than $10,000   17
38. Change in sleeping habits.   16
39. Change in number of family get-togethers.   15
40. Change in eating habits.   15
41. Vacation.   13
42. Christmas.   12
43. Minor violations of the law.   11

What Is Normal and What Isn't?

All of us will feel depressed from time to time. All of us
will feel the pain of losing a loved one, a spouse, a parent. Many
of us will feel the anxiety associated with losing a job, of being
rejected in one way or another. We mourn such losses. We
grieve. We readjust. And since some of these losses are
profound, the readjustment period may be long. This is normal.
But at times, normal grief becomes something more. It becomes
major depression. And when this happens it needs to be treated.

The Bad News and the Good News

The bad news is that there are a lot of depressed people
who don't get the help they need. Many seek help from their
family physician, who isn't really looking for depression anyway,
and their problems remain untreated. Some go to their ministers

for advice, but often they are told that they have spiritual problems they need to "work out." Others go to Christian counselors, social workers, or clinical psychologists, none of whom can prescribe medication. The upshot of all of this misdirected searching is that many people remain depressed unnecessarily.

The good news is that there is effective treatment for those with depression, but only if the condition is properly diagnosed. This book is meant not as a guide for self-diagnosis, but only to help you understand depression. This book will not cure you. Only effective treatment can bring about a cure. And such treatment consists of medication, along with psychotherapy, with the emphasis on medication. The only people qualified to give such treatment are biological psychiatrists. They are the most qualified professionals in treating depression because they understand how medications work to change "altered" brain chemistry.

PART TWO

When It Isn't Depression

2

If It Isn't Depression,
What Is It?

One evening I went down to the emergency room to see a patient named Alice, who had migratory joint pains which started in the ankles and went up to the knees. When I walked into the emergency room, with a stethoscope around my neck, everyone started to laugh. "We've never seen a psychiatrist with a stethoscope around his neck," they joked.

"It's about time you did, then," I said. And they laughed some more.

I then began to talk with the young lady, and she told me about her joint pain. I touched her ankles and knees and found them hot to the touch and very tender. She was suffering from arthritis. One medical student, two residents, and an emergency room staff physician had seen this young lady. All they had to do was touch her legs, and they would have been able to make the correct diagnosis. The trouble was they didn't.

The Importance of a Thorough Physical Exam

A good many of my colleagues do not bother to conduct their own physical exams when they hospitalize a patient but rely instead on the exams of someone else. They have distanced themselves from medicine and are probably losing their own diagnostic skills in the process. Worse yet, they are losing sight of the fact that the symptoms they see in their patients could be caused by physical illness.

In one of his many articles on the nature of psychiatry, Dr. Richard Hall argues that every patient who has an emotional symptom severe enough to warrant medical attention needs to have a good, thorough, physical exam, complete with appropriate laboratory tests. Physical illnesses are great mimickers of emotional disorders, so psychiatrists must hone their diagnostic skills if they hope to distinguish one from the other.

Let's say you go to a psychiatrist because you have been feeling tired, anxious, and a bit depressed. Your psychiatrist gives you a thorough exam and finds out that your problem is not emotional at all. You are in the first stages of cancer. If your psychiatrist had not taken the initiative in giving you a good exam or making sure you've had one, your cancer might have gone undetected for many months, by which time there might be little anyone could do for you. As it is now, you are being treated for cancer, not depression, and your physician tells you your chances of beating the disease are good. All this because your psychiatrist took the initiative.

Caroline: A Story of Misdiagnosis

I am watching the children from behind my desk. Most of them are sleeping peacefully. A few are squirming on their mats. One little boy seems to be awake, though his eyes are still closed.

I know that in a few minutes nap time will be over. I will have to get up from my desk and wake them. Then I will have to read them a story. Or maybe teach them a song. I haven't decided what I'm going to do. I don't want to decide. All I want to do is sit at my desk and rest. I am so tired. So tired. Then I think to myself, "Maybe they won't wake up right away. Maybe they will sleep through the afternoon. Oh, I hope so! I hope so!" And with that I close my eyes and pray silently for a few moments.

I am soon disappointed. Five minutes later twenty-three small children are all wide awake and sitting cross-legged on their mats and looking up at their teacher. I barely have the strength and the courage to respond to them. "What is wrong with me?" I ask myself. "What is wrong with me?"

I tell the children that it's time for a story. Slowly I get up from my desk, pick up a book, and make my way to the "reading chair."

Each step seems tremendously difficult. It's like I'm trying to walk the high wire, only I'm sure there isn't any net to catch me if I fall. I make it to the chair and sit down. My legs are trembling. My heart is racing. For a moment I feel like I am at the bottom of a deep, dark pit. I am utterly alone in absolute darkness. And then the darkness fades and I am back in the classroom with my children.

I tell myself to just relax. Breathe in and then out. In and then out. And after a couple of deep breaths, I feel a little better. I open the book and begin to read about Katie the caboose, but after only a few minutes I am unable to focus on the words. Each page is a jumble of nonsense. A couple more deep breaths, and I try again, but still the words make no sense.

What is happening here? Why can't I read a simple story? I try again, but it only gets worse. I feel like I am falling into the darkness of the pit once more.

The next thing I know I'm standing up and shouting at my children. I have never shouted at my children before. Not like this. Not in twenty-seven years of teaching. But there I am. Shouting about how little respect they have for the people around them and what kind of families do they come from that they learned to behave this way and on and on and on.

What are you doing? Why are you shouting like this? Can't you see you're frightening your children? Can't you see you're frightening yourself? Stop it! Stop it! Stop it! And I try to stop myself, but I can't. The shouting continues. I don't know why. It's like my body has been taken over by something else, something alien. I don't know what to do.

And then all of a sudden the shouting stops, and I look at the

*small faces staring up at me, some of them tear-stained, some
bewildered, and there is nothing I can say so I run from the classroom
and down the hall to the teachers' lounge. And when I sit down on the
sofa by the Coke machine, I burst into tears.*

A Personal History

Caroline was forty-nine years old, the mother of three
boys, and a grandmother. She had taught kindergarten for
twenty-seven years. She always considered herself a happy
person and always enjoyed life. "I'm not trying to say I've never
had to struggle," she told me. "When you raise three children, a
little bit of struggle is inevitable. But I always believed God was
watching over me and that if I kept my faith, everything would
work out for the best. I never expected anything like this."

Caroline had already been to two other psychiatrists.
Neither was able to help. Then again, neither had bothered
with laboratory studies or insisted on a physical exam. The only
question they asked her was if she had ever suffered from any
major illnesses. If they had taken a little more initiative, they
could have saved Caroline from a lot of pain.

Caroline's "depression" began about two months after she
had had a hysterectomy. At first she didn't realize anything was
wrong. She started moping around the house. She didn't seem
to be interested in much of anything, but she figured she was just
going through a hormonal change as a result of the surgery and
that she'd adjust soon enough. When she didn't seem to get
better, she went back to her doctor and he prescribed an
estrogen pill. The pill didn't work.

"I began to think I would never be happy again," she told
me. "I didn't understand what was happening to me, so I went
to see my doctor again, but all I did was cry." Caroline's doctor
recommended that she see a psychiatrist, which she did. Two
months later she lost control of her feelings in front of her
kindergarten class and began shouting.

Many times we assume that only one problem exists when

we see a patient with a certain set of symptoms. Caroline was clearly upset. She was irritable, anxious, and she was beginning to have trouble falling asleep. The two psychiatrists she went to both assumed she was depressed solely because she had some of the symptoms of major depression. They didn't look any further, so they failed to see that the cause of Caroline's pain was something physical. Caroline was depressed, but her emotional distress was caused by a hormonal imbalance, which is why antidepressants didn't work. I recommended she see an endocrinologist, someone who specializes in hormonal disorders, and one week later she did. Her new doctor, her fifth in eight months, put her on an estrogen patch. The patch allowed more estrogen into her bloodstream than the estrogen pill had, and now she is feeling just fine.

The Fair Oaks System

In his book, *Good News About Depression*, Dr. Mark Gold lists what the psychiatrists at Fair Oaks Hospital do to rule out physical illness as a cause of emotional problems.[1] First, they conduct a detailed personal history of the patient, including the patient's family history. This information gives some clues as to what is going on with the patient.

Next, they examine the patient's mental status, which gives clues as to how the patient is feeling emotionally. This exam involves talking with the patient, asking questions about how he feels, observing his actions and facial expressions, and administering simple tests of his memory and reasoning capabilities. When I conduct a mental status exam, I also talk to the relatives of the patient. They often provide information about the patient which the patient cannot or will not provide.

Finally, Fair Oaks Hospital conducts a complete physical and neurological exam. When these are complete, the patient is given a complete endocrine and laboratory exam. These last two examinations are important to determine if the patient's problem has a physical cause. Not only do they conduct routine blood and urine tests, but they will also administer a series of drug screens, heavy metal screens, vitamin screens, special lab tests, and neuroendocrine studies.

Does everyone who suffers from depression need this type of workup? No. But if the depressed patient has not responded to treatment, then this type of workup is necessary.

The Mind and the Body: A Holistic View

If Caroline's story can teach us anything, it is that physical health and emotional health are related. Emotions influence how our hearts and stomachs work; just as how what happens within our hearts and stomachs influences how we feel. The mind and the body work together and are, in fact, inseparable. It is only natural, then, that problems in one area cause problems in another. This was the case with Caroline. This is also why it is important that we know a little about how our hormones work—which is the subject of our next chapter.

— 3 —

It's All in the Glands

You are walking home around ten o'clock in the evening. You hear footsteps somewhere behind you. You turn down a side street, and the sound of the footsteps follows. You quicken your pace, and though you don't look behind to see who is there, every one of your senses is alert. You are ready for anything.

What is happening here? Your glands are taking over, giving you the energy and the strength you need to meet any potential danger, even if it is only imaginary. The truth is, you wouldn't be able to do much of anything if it weren't for your glands, for they help regulate how your body performs and develops. Your glands secrete hormones which determine many things about you: how tall you are, your temperature, your energy level, your blood pressure and your heart rate, your appetite, even your desire to sleep in the middle of the afternoon. All in all, your glands are part of a complex system, what we call the endocrine system, which tries to maintain a constant internal environment.

The Hypothalamus: Like a Thermostat

If your house has central heat and air, it also has a thermostat which keeps track of the temperature. When your house is too cold, the thermostat relays this information to the furnace, which then starts blowing warm air through the ducts. Same thing when it's too hot, only you get cool air. When the temperature in your house reaches the temperature registered on your thermostat, the thermostat tells the system to shut down. Regulating the temperature inside your house is an on-again, off-again, on-again process.

This same process is the operating principle of your endocrine system, though on a much more complex scale. Instead of regulating temperature alone, your body must regulate all of your metabolic functions. It would be as if your thermostat regulated not only the temperature inside your house, but let you know when your refrigerator was empty, when the laundry needed to be washed, when you needed to fill up your car with gas, and anything else you might need to do. What kind of thermostat is capable of all this? It's called the hypothalamus.

The hypothalamus is at the base of the brain directly above the pituitary gland. Though it is but the size of a pea, it keeps track of everything your glands are and are not doing. When word gets back to the hypothalamus, for example, that there isn't enough thyroid in the blood, it sends a message (via a thyroid-releasing hormone) to the pituitary gland to produce more thyroid-stimulating hormone, which then stimulates the thyroid to do its job. When enough of the thyroid hormone has been produced, the hypothalamus senses this and stops sending the thyroid-releasing hormone. The production of the thyroid hormone stops soon after.

As the thermostat of your endocrine system, your hypothalamus controls the hormone production for every endocrine gland in your body: the pituitary, the thyroid, the adrenals, the pancreas, and a few more besides. This direct control enables the hypothalamus to keep your entire endocrine system in balance.

When Something Goes Wrong

When something goes wrong with your endocrine system, when your glands secrete too much of one kind of hormone or not enough of another, then you begin to act and feel differently. Like Caroline, you begin to feel as if something alien has taken control of your body. But often it is difficult to determine whether the change in hormones is the cause of your emotional distress or vice versa. Are your physical ailments the cause of your depression? Or is it the other way around? The truth is that diseases of the endocrine system mimic depression. The only way we can judge what is really going on is to order the right laboratory exams when appropriate.

Problems with the Pituitary

An old man was admitted to the emergency room of a major metropolitan hospital. He appeared to be depressed. He also appeared to be suffering from delusions. He said his name was Jake.

The hospital staff kept Jake overnight so they could run some tests. Jake didn't have a problem with this, but then he was barely aware of what was happening to him. The next morning one of the nurses found Jake crawling on the floor beneath his bed. He asked her if she could pick up one of the little bottles on the floor. Apparently he "saw" small bottles of liquor on the floor beneath his hospital bed. He also saw them on the window sill of his room, but whenever he reached for them they vanished. He became quite upset over the imaginary bottles and soon began to cry. The nurse helped him into bed, and he fell asleep.

Was Jake severely depressed? Was he psychotic? Was he an alcoholic suffering from withdrawal? He certainly appeared so, but his condition was actually the result of a problem with his pituitary known as hyponatremia. Jake's apparent depression was due to the lack of sodium in his bloodstream. The hospital staff put Jake on a high-sodium diet. They also limited his fluids. In two weeks he was much better.

How the Pituitary Works

The pituitary gland is attached to the base of the brain just below the hypothalamus. It sends groups of hormones to the various glands (the thyroid, the adrenals, the sex glands) throughout the body in order to keep the systems of the body running smoothly. The pituitary is also a part of the limbic system (a structure of the brain), which has a profound effect on our emotional stability. This means your pituitary is linked to how you feel, whether good or bad. If there is something wrong with your pituitary gland, you will experience emotional problems as well as physical problems.

Pituitary Disorders

Panhypopituitarism. This condition occurs when all of the hormones of the pituitary gland shut down, an abnormality usually caused by a tumor. The thyroid and the adrenal glands are both affected, as are the ovaries and the testes. If you suffer from panhypopituitarism, you often appear to be depressed. As the condition progresses, you may also experience thyroid problems, anxiety, and sexual dysfunction, among other things. Treatment commonly involves replacing gland-stimulating hormones. In some cases, surgery is required.

Acromegaly. This condition occurs in children when the pituitary gland produces too much growth hormone. Children so afflicted become giants and can grow to be seven or eight feet tall. The bones enlarge, especially those of the face, arms, hands, and feet. Emotional symptoms usually accompany this condition. Treatment usually involves surgery or radiation.

Hyponatremia. This condition occurs when the pituitary gland secretes a hormone which causes the kidney to retain too much water. The excess water adds to the volume of blood and dilutes the level of sodium in the bloodstream. This drop in the sodium level can cause mental confusion as well as depression. This was the case with Jake. Treatment involves a combination of restricting fluids and adding salt to the diet.

Problems with the Thyroid

One evening a thirty-four-year-old white female was admitted to the psychiatric ward of the Louisville General Hospital. She said her name was Mrs. Storm. She was definitely psychotic. She heard voices, was more than a little paranoid, and looked like she was suffering from either schizophrenia or a manic depressive psychosis. We gave her thorazine for her psychotic state and she responded to it rather quickly. In a few days she was no longer bothered by voices and was no longer delusional. And since this was the first time she had heard these voices and had delusions, we felt that she was suffering from bipolar illness (see Chapter 6).

We ordered a thyroid profile on her, and the results indicated a thyroid deficiency, so we began to give her a thyroid hormone, along with her antipsychotic. In ten days she was discharged from the hospital. She received follow-up treatment as an out-patient in the hospital clinic. The dose of her antipsychotic was reduced progressively until she was off the drug completely. Since then, she has kept taking her thyroid hormone and has remained symptom-free. The truth was Mrs. Storm's psychotic episode stemmed from a thyroid problem.

Almost two weeks after we treated and discharged Mrs. Storm, another woman was admitted to our ward. She said her name was Mrs. Jeffries. She was depressed and seemed suicidal. She hadn't been sleeping very well, had lost her appetite as well as fifteen pounds, and had no energy. Life was just one big chore. She looked very sad. We did a thyroid study on her as well and found that she too had a thyroid deficiency, so we started her on an antidepressant, as well as hormone therapy. In fifteen days we discharged her from the hospital. As was the case with Mrs. Storm, Mrs. Jeffries also received follow-up treatment as an out-patient in the clinic.

Why Thyroid Studies Are Important

Some patients who suffer from thyroid illness also suffer from various forms of depression and fatigue. This is particularly true of women. But not everyone with a thyroid problem is depressed. Both Mrs. Storm and Mrs. Jeffries had thyroid problems, and both responded to hormone replacement. If we hadn't done the thyroid studies on them, we wouldn't have been able to help them.

Many people with thyroid problems are judged depressed simply because they exhibit the symptoms of depression. Some might even exhibit psychotic symptoms. The truth is that if your thyroid malfunctions, so do you. If your thyroid releases too much thyroid hormone into your bloodstream (hyperthyroidism), you will become restless, irritable, and anxious, and you will also be subject to mood swings. Not enough (hypothyroidism), and you will feel worn out and tired most of the time. You will have great trouble doing even the simplest of mental tasks. What does this tell us? Simply this: a proper examination of the thyroid can be very helpful in any evaluation of mental illness.

Problems with the Adrenal Glands

Candice had been suffering from depression and had had psychotic symptoms for over two years. She had been to three other doctors before she came to me, and they all told her the same thing: that her depression and psychosis were triggered by the death of her son. The boy, only eight years old at the time, had been killed as he crossed in front of his school bus. The driver never saw him.

However, I found that Candice was not suffering from

depression, but from a disease of the adrenal glands known as Cushing's Syndrome, a disease which can mimic depression, and which can become quite serious if not treated. Fortunately, she received the proper treatment. In her case the tumors causing her condition were surgically removed, and she is now doing fine.

How the Adrenal Glands Work

The adrenal glands have a number of functions because they are really two glands in one: the medulla and the cortex. The medulla secretes two hormones, norepinephrine and epinephrine, which cause the body to go into a "fight or flight" state of alertness. These hormones also act as messengers in the nervous system and carry messages from one nerve to another. The cortex secretes a variety of hormones which regulate the amount of sodium reabsorbed by the kidneys, as well as the level of sugar in the blood. When there is something wrong with the way these glands function, when there is too much or not enough of these hormones, then you can expect to suffer from severe emotional distress.

Diseases of the Adrenal Glands

Addison's disease. This somewhat rare condition occurs when the adrenals produce too little cortisol. Consequently, the gland fails. This disease is often associated with symptoms of depression. If you suffer from Addison's disease, you may feel unusually weak and tired. You will be short of breath, and have low blood pressure. You will also have little appetite. And if you have an especially serious case, you may become psychotic. Treatment is simple. Hormonal replacement therapy does the trick in most instances.

Cushing's syndrome. This condition is just the opposite of Addison's disease and occurs when the adrenal cortex produces too much cortisol, an abnormality usually caused by tumors of the adrenal gland. If you have this condition you will probably suffer from depression, and you may become grossly psychotic. Treatment involves either surgery or radiation therapy.

Pheochromocytoma. This is a very rare illness which every medical student and resident looks for, though few find. Pheochromocytoma are tumors most often of the adrenal medulla. If you have these tumors you may exhibit many of the symptoms associated with depression and anxiety, and you may be especially vulnerable to panic attacks. Some patients have reportedly suffered from psychotic episodes. Treatment involves surgery, which solves the problem in most cases.

Diabetes

When Eric was in college, he stood six foot four and weighed a muscular 210 pounds. He played tight-end on the football team and was a forward on the basketball team. Now, at thirty-three, he weighed close to 300 pounds. His buddies kidded him about watching too much football and drinking too much beer, but Eric did little of either.

On weekdays he dragged himself to work at a major insurance company and hid out in his office. On weekends he mostly sat around the house. Eric complained of being tired all the time, but he also had trouble sleeping. He would wake up three or four times a night, and when he couldn't fall back to sleep, he would head for the kitchen and eat a ham sandwich or a piece of pie. Eric's wife thought he was depressed and urged him to see a psychiatrist. Eric agreed.

As you have probably guessed by now, Eric was not suffering from depression. He was in a great deal of emotional pain, but his pain was caused by a hormonal imbalance. Eric had Type II diabetes. I advised Eric's physician of his condition, and he immediately put Eric on a restricted diet and a daily exercise program. If Eric hadn't improved, which is sometimes the case, his physician would have given him some antidiabetic medication to supplement the diet and the exercise. But Eric did improve. He lost fifty pounds. He no longer felt so tired. And he no longer seemed depressed.

Diabetes or Depression?

When your pancreas does not produce enough insulin, or when the cells of your body can't use the insulin which is produced, high levels of glucose remain in your bloodstream. This forces your body to metabolize fats and proteins instead of glucose to produce energy. The result is diabetes, though the symptoms may mimic those of depression.

If you suffer from Type I diabetes, often called insulin-dependent diabetes, you will experience a variety of symptoms ranging from excessive thirst and frequent urination to excessive hunger and dramatic weight loss. Among the other symptoms you might experience are blurred vision, increasing weakness, lethargy, difficulty sleeping, and confusion. You may also develop the symptoms of major depression. Type I diabetes is treated with insulin injections. People who develop this condition do so before the age of thirty.

If you suffer from Type II diabetes, your body still produces insulin, but not enough. You feel weak and tired because you are not getting all of the energy you need, and so you overeat in order to compensate. The more you eat, the more sugar enters your blood, and the more insulin you need to break it down. Since your body is not producing enough insulin in the first place, the deficiency of insulin in your blood becomes greater and greater, and the more you need to eat. You continue to feel weak and tired. You may have trouble sleeping. As time goes on, you may become confused. You may also develop symptoms usually associated with psychiatric illness.

Hypoglycemia

A young woman appeared in the square of a downtown mall and began dancing and singing. Some of the shoppers stopped to watch, thinking she was a street performer. But as the young woman continued to dance and sing, her movements became wilder and wilder. Soon she was out of control, bumping into people in the square, cursing under her breath, laughing hysterically. The mall security restrained her quickly and then called for the police. "She's out of her mind," they said. "A complete schizo." The police took the woman to the emergency room of a university hospital.

The young woman's name was Rachel. She was twenty-nine, and she was an insulin-dependent diabetic. She was not "crazy" or "schizo." Her "schizophrenic" dancing episode was the result of taking too much insulin, which caused her blood-sugar level to drop, thereby triggering a hypoglycemic reaction.

The World of the Hypoglycemic

Hypoglycemia is the opposite of diabetes, and though it usually occurs in diabetics, it also appears in nondiabetics. Some patients with this condition may appear to be suffering from bipolar illness, experiencing the delusions, the hallucinations, and the excitement associated with an acute psychotic state. This was the case with Rachel. Others may seem depressed, anxious, or even demented. They may complain of feeling faint, of feeling shaky or weak, or of having headaches. In the most serious cases, patients who suffer from hypoglycemia may go into a coma and die.

There was a time when every woman who complained of being lightheaded was diagnosed as suffering from hypoglycemia. Those days are gone, but for those who do suffer from hypoglycemia, proper treatment can be critical. It is also simple. Patients respond to diet regulation, eating high-protein snacks and meals five times a day rather than three, and cutting back on sugary foods. If they feel an attack coming on, they need to drink some fruit juice. And if they become unconscious, they need a glucose injection as soon as possible. When I was an intern, anyone who came to the hospital in a comatose state received glucose in his or her veins. Some of those patients woke up shortly thereafter because their comas had been caused by hypoglycemia.

The Psychiatrist as Detective

In order to figure out whether a patient has a thyroid problem or a pituitary problem or any other glandular problem rather than depression, psychiatrists have to be good detectives. Like any good detective we have to have a high degree of suspicion. We have to look carefully at the clues before we rule out one cause or another. This means considering everything from basic symptoms to family histories to laboratory test results.

Let's say a patient comes into my office and tells me she has been depressed for five years, has been in and out of countless psychiatric offices, has tried a number of different medications, and nothing has worked. I would order a variety of laboratory tests to see if the cause of her depression was physical.

This doesn't mean I order elaborate tests for all of my patients. But it does mean I pay close attention to detail. I have to be persistent. I can't just give my patients some antidepressants and hope for the best simply because they appear depressed. There are many different causes of depression. Since I am a detective, I have to keep looking until I find the one cause that fits the clues.

Sometimes the cause of depression is external—the result of taking legal or illegal drugs. We will look at how drugs affect our mental state in the next chapter.

4

Drugs and Depression

On June 19, 1986, shortly after being drafted by the Boston Celtics, a basketball player named Len Bias died as a result of taking cocaine. At the 1988 Olympic games in Seoul, South Korea, the Canadian sprinter Ben Johnson was stripped of his gold medal because he had used anabolic steroids while training. Players in both the NFL and the NBA have been suspended, even banned for life, because they have taken drugs. But in spite of all of the negative press drugs have received, ours is still a quick-fix society which views drugs, in all their many forms, as an almost indispensable part of the "good life."

Drugs—legal and illegal—are everywhere, on the street, in the bars, in the drugstores (excuse the obvious) and supermarkets, and in the offices of physicians. If you turn on your television on any given night, you are bound to see commercials praising the virtues of one drug or another. We buy aspirin and other pain relievers because they bring us immediate relief. We buy beer (alcohol is a potent drug) because we equate it with healthy, successful men and women playing volleyball on the beach. We buy one kind of pill to help us sleep at night and another kind to get us going again in the morning. We cannot imagine a world without drugs.

In spite of the prevalence of drugs in our society, most of us are not fully aware of just what the drugs we take can do. All drugs influence the biochemistry of the body in some way. Many drugs act directly upon the brain. It almost goes without saying that drugs can affect our emotions, even drugs prescribed for us by our physicians. Drugs, like those physical illnesses which mimic depression, can also cause many of the symptoms associated with emotional and mental illness.

Addicted to Marijuana

His name was Tripp. He was fifteen, had longish, brown hair, and was dressed in green slacks, a yellow button-down shirt, untucked, and a green and red tie. His mother, a petite woman in her forties, brought him to my office. She told me Tripp had become violent lately, both at school and at home, and over seemingly trivial matters. She also told me that his grades had dropped dramatically during the last year, that he had stopped seeing his friends, and that he spent most of his time just sitting in front of the television. She believed, and not without some cause, that her son was depressed. "If I didn't know him better," she said, "I'd think he was a druggie."

Tripp was in no mood to talk about anything and sat stiffly in the chair across from me. He was quite angry. But after ten minutes of silence, he began to respond to my questions.

"This wasn't my idea," he said. "It was hers."

I nodded.

"She's always trying to get me to do things. 'Do your homework Tripp,'" he mimicked. "'Do the lawn, Tripp. Why don't you try out for the soccer team this year? I think you'd be wonderful.'"

Obviously Tripp and his mother did not get along very well. I asked him if he knew why his mother had brought him to see me, but he only shrugged his shoulders. Then he told me he had always been an average student but that his mother expected him to make the Dean's list. He didn't like sports, but he did like music. He didn't take drugs and he didn't drink beer. "Except once," he added. "I was twelve and it was the Fourth of July and me and a friend of mine got really drunk. The worst part was trying to bike home. I must have thrown up three times on the way, and when I did get home I told myself never again."

I asked Tripp to come in some time during the next week for some tests, a blood test and a urine test, among others, and he agreed, though a bit reluctantly. Almost every test came back normal, with one exception. The lab found a significant amount of THC in Tripp's urine, which meant that Tripp had been smoking marijuana for some time, and heavily at that.

During our next session I asked Tripp if he had ever tried marijuana. At first he became angry and said he wasn't into that kind of thing, but after a few minutes he began to talk about himself more openly. For the past two years he had been smoking three or four joints a day, one or two in the morning, before school, and a couple more in the afternoon. At first it was a "buddy thing," as he put it. He and his friends thought it great fun to get together and smoke. Theirs was an exclusive, "members only" club. But after several months or so, Tripp found himself lighting up without his friends. He became more and more of a loner, his schoolwork started to slide, and by the time he turned fifteen, he didn't have any friends. He wasn't interested in doing much of anything. He just didn't care.

After a month of meeting with Tripp once a week, I convinced him of the need to give up smoking, and, just as important, the need to get involved with people his own age. He started going to Young Life meetings, a Christian program designed for young people, and soon he was going to meetings and getting to know new friends.

Two months after Tripp stopped smoking marijuana, his "depression" disappeared. The change was dramatic. The last time I spoke with Tripp he told me he was going to try out for the soccer team at his school.

Addicted to Cocaine

John was thirty-six and tall, with reddish hair. He had been married for sixteen years, but he and his wife had no children. Two years before I knew John, he started using cocaine. He couldn't really say why he started, he just did. One Thursday night, he and three friends from work went looking for a good time. One of his friends brought along some cocaine.

When John came to see me, he certainly looked depressed. He had been "drug free" for about six weeks, but he was visibly sad and seemed to lack any energy whatsoever. His head drooped, and he rarely looked me in the eye when he spoke. He said he was unable to motivate himself any more. He couldn't concentrate on the most mundane things. Life just wasn't any fun. He also said he was having problems with his wife.

When John's wife found out about his cocaine use, she was angry and disillusioned. She even threatened to leave her husband. But John's cocaine use hadn't caused this friction between the two of them. They had been having a hard time for years. In fact, the previous Christmas his wife had left him for three weeks. She had gone to Jamaica with two of her friends and hadn't even bothered to drop him a postcard. They got back together, but they still had their problems. And the cocaine only made things worse.

I felt that John was suffering from major depression, and since he had been using cocaine, I started him on Norpramin, a tricyclic antidepressant, which reportedly helps cocaine addicts control their cravings. Everything was going fine for a while. John seemed to be regaining his motivation and his concentration. He and his wife were beginning to talk about their problems. And then one night John went out once again with his cocaine buddies and got high. His wife was devastated. And for John, it was like starting from square one.

John's depression was real. It was also made worse by his cocaine use. He would feel "real" good when he was high, but when he came down he would sink even further into depression. The more he used cocaine, the worse his depression became. Eventually, his wife, Heather, did pack up and leave. She lived with her mother in Miami until John got his life back together.

The Truth About Illegal Drugs

Drugs have a profound effect on our emotional and mental state-of-being. This is as true of illegal drugs as it is for over-the-counter medication. The various symptoms created by using illegal drugs mimic those of every major emotional illness. And yet no matter how serious the consequences, many people who use illegal drugs try to downplay the effect those drugs can have on their lives. This is especially true of those who come to a psychiatrist for help. Patients often hide their illegal drug use from their psychiatrists. Some may be embarrassed or even feel ashamed. Some may simply refuse to admit that drugs are harmful.

"I only drink on the weekends."

"A joint every other day won't hurt."

"It's not like I'm doing coke at the office. I mean I'm not addicted or anything."

Not everyone who uses illegal drugs will develop symptoms which mimic those of emotional illness. Not everyone who is emotionally ill uses illegal drugs. But since such drug use can cause the symptoms of emotional illness, psychiatrists need to be able to determine the truth. Whenever I suspect a patient of having a drug problem, I order a urine test. This test provides a good deal of information about a patient's drug use and is often helpful in those hard-to-diagnose cases. Sometimes, as was the case with Tripp, patients find that their "depression" disappears once they stop using drugs. In other cases, as we saw with John, the recovery process may be more complicated. Whatever the circumstances, it is important to find out what drug the patient is using. Without this knowledge, effective treatment is impossible.

Which Drugs Cause Which Symptoms?

Cocaine. If you use cocaine, your brain will become more and more active until you enter a manic or euphoric state. While intoxicated, you will become hyperactive, with feelings of exaggerated self-confidence bordering on delusions of grandeur. Further symptoms may include irritability, anxiety, depression, paranoia, and even delirium. Some users may appear to be suffering from a mania or a full-blown psychosis. Others may exhibit delusions similar to those exhibited by schizophrenics. Once the initial rush of increased brain activity is over, you will lose your sense of euphoria and become depressed, anxious, and fatigued.

Marijuana. If you use marijuana, you may experience a sense of euphoria similar to that experienced by those who use cocaine. You may also become depressed. You may even become psychotic.

Narcotics. If you use drugs like heroin or morphine, you will not feel pain, for these drugs prevent pain sensations from registering. When you stop using these drugs, you will experience withdrawal. Common symptoms of withdrawal include restlessness, intense craving, anxiety, and even depression. Although the acute phase of your withdrawal will last only seven to ten days, you may suffer from sleep problems and mood changes for many months.

Psychedelic Drugs. If you use psychedelic drugs, you will probably suffer from some kind of hallucination. You may see bright, vivid images, or hear strange, compelling voices. You may become paranoid and deluded. Once your psychotic experience is over, you may become depressed.

When the Problem Is Alcohol

According to some estimates, forty percent of all alcoholics suffer from depression, and many also suffer from anxiety disorders and panic attacks. When I talk with suffering alcoholics, I ask them why they drink. They often tell me they drink because they like the euphoric feeling drinking produces. They drink to forget about their problems. They drink because it calms them. They drink because it lifts them out of their depressions, at least for a while. And when the effect of the alcohol wears off, all they need to recapture that euphoria, to lift them once again out of their depression, is to take another drink.

The Case of Kristina

A thirty-five-year-old woman walked into my office. She was short and thin, with long, black hair and blue eyes. She wore a black skirt with a matching jacket. She sat down in the chair across from me and took off her sunglasses, also black. Her name was Kristina, and she suffered from alcoholism. She was also depressed.

"I just don't know what to say," she said.

"What happened?"

"I just don't know. I remember rounding the curve, and then the next thing I know there are three cars in the ditch."

"Were you drinking?"

Kristina did not answer me at first. She looked to the wall, she bit her lip, and then she nodded her head slowly and looked at me. Then she began to cry.

I treated Kristina for depression for some months, but she didn't get any better. I tried to get her to take her medication, but she resisted. I tried to get her to attend some AA meetings, but she just made excuses. The problem was that she didn't think her drinking was a problem. She thought she could handle any amount of alcohol. Unfortunately, she was wrong. Sometimes, she came to my office drunk. One day her husband, Pete, called to tell me that Kristina had boarded a plane for New York. She had no money, and no one was waiting at the airport to pick her up. Pete flew up an hour later and found her sleeping in the corner of an airport bar. She was dead drunk, and had probably been drunk for hours.

Whenever Kristina drinks, and she drinks a lot, she makes a wreck of her life. The accident she described above was her second major accident in four weeks. Both accidents occurred in the middle of the afternoon. In both cases Kristina had been drinking heavily. Fortunately, no one was hurt in either accident, though Kristina totaled her car in the second. Of much greater concern is the fact that in both of these accidents, Kristina was driving her kids home from school. She is a tragedy waiting to happen.

What About Prescription Drugs?

Medications prescribed by physicians can also cause emotional or psychological problems in some patients. All such medications have definite side-effects (more about side effects in Chapter 11). Some prescription drugs may cause a toxic reaction, and many have multiple effects on the body. Many of these drugs also affect the way your brain functions—everything from how you react to pain to how much sleep you think you need. Once again, before I can help you, I need to know what medications you are on and how much you are taking.

One big problem with prescription drugs is that many people take too many at the same time. They are overmedicated. Let me give one example. I was asked to evaluate the mental and emotional condition of a seventy-eight-year-old woman living in a nursing home. She was very lethargic. Her eyes were half-closed. And as I talked with her I realized that she was barely aware of what was going on around her. She didn't look at me the whole time I was with her. Her speech was slurred. She couldn't answer even the simplest of questions I put to her.

What was wrong with this woman? Was there anything I

could do to help her? She certainly looked depressed. She had all the signs of dementia and depression. Then I looked at her chart and saw that she was on twenty different medications. No wonder she was so lethargic. No wonder she looked depressed. I immediately took her off all medication. Within a couple of weeks she had brightened up considerably. She still has a few problems, but she is much more aware, much more able to cope with her life. She is also much happier.

I've had some patients sent to me who were taking an antipsychotic, an antidepressant, an antianxiety agent, and a sleeping pill, all at the same time. Some of these patients need a two-week washout period. They need to wash the medication out of their system so we can better determine just what medication they really need. I am often amazed by what happens next. Some of these patients lose their listlessness. They begin to perk up, begin to think more clearly, and begin to enjoy life once again.

I am not saying that most older patients do not need their medications. I am simply saying that I need to know what medications my patients are on, how much they are taking, and why they take them. If I put my patients on yet another drug without understanding the dynamics of the drugs they are already on, I could make matters worse.

Summing Up

We have seen how depression may be the result of physical problems, such as pituitary or thyroid disorders, or the result of using drugs—both legal and illegal. We have determined when the problem is *not* depression. Now we will answer the next, inevitable question: "How do you know when it *is* depression?"

PART THREE

When It Is Depression

— 5 —

Depression: A Thousand Faces

Did you ever see the movie *Man of a Thousand Faces*? It's the story of the actor Lon Chaney and his rise to stardom. At a very early age, Lon Chaney learned to be very expressive because both of his parents were deaf and mute. This expressiveness, plus a great skill at applying makeup, made him the consummate actor. Every time Chaney played a different character, he wore a new face. Soon he came to be known as the man with a thousand faces.

Depression is the Lon Chaney of the medical world: one disease, but a thousand faces. There are different types of depression which may appear at various times in our lives. Their symptoms differ, and they are even treated differently. In the next several chapters, we will look at some of the "faces" or types of depression, including major depression, dysthymic disorder, atypical depression, manic depression, cyclothymia, psychotic depression, and schizoaffective disorder. We will also examine the categories of depression that strike three groups of people: women, children, and the elderly.

Major Depression

Marie: A Story of Major Depression

I am awake, but I do not open my eyes. I will not open my eyes. Not yet. I'm not ready. I lie in bed a while and wonder what time it is. It must be ten in the morning. Feels like a ten-o'clock sun. I can feel the sharp, bright sun shining through the windows of my bedroom. I hate it! It's like a thousand little spears jabbing at me saying, "Wake up! Wake up! Get out of bed! There's things to do! Places to go!" Only it's not that simple.

Sometimes it takes me all morning to get out of bed. The sun doesn't help. It only makes things worse. Why can't Harry just leave the shades down? He knows what it's like for me. I'll get up sooner or later. Why does he have to force the issue by raising those shades? I roll over and bury my head under my pillow, under the sheets. Suddenly the sun is gone and I am surrounded by darkness. I tell myself it'll be hours before I need to think about getting up. Then I fall back to sleep.

I sleep for a couple of hours. Maybe longer. Then I open my eyes, slowly, look around the room. Everything seems darker. I wonder what has become of the sun and those thousand little spears. Why is there no sun? Then I realize that the sun has moved to the other side of the house. Half the day is gone, and I am just now getting out of bed. I wonder if I should get dressed so I look in my closet, but I can't decide what I should wear. I throw on my bathrobe and head for the kitchen.

I don't seem to notice what a wreck the house is. The floors haven't been swept in weeks. The furniture hasn't been dusted in twice that. The dishes need washing. So does the laundry. There are books and papers scattered all over the place. I don't seem to notice. Maybe I don't care. I walk down the hallway stepping over piles of dirty clothes.

I don't remember the last time I did the laundry. Seems like there's always piles of dirty clothes about. Harry will get to it soon enough. Soon as he runs out of underwear. Then I forget about the laundry and I find myself standing in front of the pantry and staring at a few boxes of cereal, a bag of rice, and some Oreo cookies. I don't feel much like cereal. The same with the rice. I grab the Oreos, head for the couch, and flick on the TV. By the time I finish the Oreos it's after three. I'm watching some old movie but I can't figure out what's going on. I turn it off. I stare at the blank and silent screen and wonder what I'm going to do for the rest of the afternoon. Maybe I could go for a walk. I could use some fresh air. No, that would mean I'd have to get dressed. Too much trouble.

The longer I sit on the couch, the more I become aware of my own inability to get off the couch, to get on with my life. What is wrong with me? Why am I like this? I can't go on like this forever. What am I going to do? Before I can ask myself another question, I curl up on the couch and begin to cry.

I have absolutely no control over this. I seem to cry as naturally and as unconsciously as most people breathe. And yet I am aware of a tremendous sense of loss. A personal loss. I can't really explain what it is. I don't have the words. But I know I have lost something important. When my husband comes home in the evening I am still there, still crying. I don't even hear him come through the door.

Woman at a Loss for Words

When Andrea first came into my office, she didn't speak for the first twenty minutes or so. It took me two or three visits before I began to get a clear picture of what she had been going through.

Andrea was twenty-three, a Christian, and newly married. She was a striking young woman, tall, with curly brown hair and green eyes behind tortoiseshell glasses. She wore a navy blue jacket with matching skirt. She was also very quiet, almost subdued, for she had put up with what she called "dog days" ever since she went away to college.

Andrea's depression started during the first semester of her freshman year. She became quite moody, and by the middle of the winter felt completely out of touch with the world. Sometimes things were so bad she would just lie down on her bed and cry. Her friends tried to make her feel better, but there was nothing they could do. They had no idea why she was crying. By the end of her sophomore year she could not function at all, and she spent most of each week in bed. She rarely attended classes, and when the year was over, she withdrew from school and moved back in with her parents.

Andrea knew all along there was something wrong with her, but she had been brought up to believe that her faith in Jesus Christ would help her to pull herself together. She believed it was better to suffer in silence than to ask for help. But when her faith wasn't enough, she became confused. By the time she came to see me, she had almost no self-esteem.

"I thought maybe I wasn't a true Christian," she told me.

I had heard this before. Many of my patients feel they are spiritually inadequate because they are depressed. "Why did you think that?" I asked.

"Well, I prayed and I prayed, only it didn't work," she said. "I was still depressed. I thought maybe I needed to join a Bible study group to help strengthen my faith. But I never told anyone about my problems. I didn't think I could. I sort of thought Jesus was testing me and in order to pass the test I had to go it alone."

I smiled at Andrea. "You don't have to go it alone," I said. "No one does."

Symptoms of Major Depression

You've probably heard that depressed people have trouble sleeping. That they don't feel like eating. That they just sit around and cry a lot. Some depressed people do suffer from these particular symptoms, but not all. Some of my patients sleep all the time. Some can't stop eating. And some show no emotion whatsoever. Two patients may have the exact opposite symptoms, and yet both of them may suffer from major depression (see chart on page 62). No patient suffers from every possible symptom. Symptoms vary from one patient to the next, and that fact raises some important questions. Where do we draw the line between eating too much and not eating enough? What is the right amount of sleep for someone who isn't depressed? In other words, what exactly is major depression and what isn't?

If you look closely at the people actually suffering from this disease, one thing sticks out in your mind: they seem to lack energy. Most of the patients I have treated for major depression, no matter what other symptoms they may have, are unable to do many of the things they once did with comparative ease. They are listless, unmotivated, unable to concentrate. They have been robbed of their ability to enjoy life.

I Can't Even Write Out a Grocery List!

Andrea's husband, David, knew about her crying episodes and moodiness, but he thought it was all just "a female thing," as he put it. He had no idea what was wrong, but he soon learned that Andrea was incapable of doing many of the things most of us take for granted. If David wanted the dishes washed, he usually had to do them himself. If he wanted the laundry done, he had to go to the laundromat. After their first year of marriage, he became quite frustrated. He told me things were so bad that Andrea couldn't even write out a grocery list. She couldn't remember what she and David needed from the store. She couldn't even remember what they had eaten the night before. Her mind would simply go blank. After a while she gave up altogether and David had to do the shopping as well.

Andrea suffers from major depression. She has little energy and zero motivation. She also has difficulty concentrating, which is why she is unable to do something as simple as writing out a grocery list. When faced with making a decision, any kind of decision, her mind goes blank.

This is one of the things that makes major depression so terrible, so destructive, this inability to cope with life. You find yourself letting things slide. You don't get as much done as you used to, and after a while, you don't care. You begin to lose your faith in God and in yourself. All you can think of is how hopeless your life is.

MAJOR DEPRESSIVE EPISODES

I. If you are suffering from major depression, your symptoms will be as follows:

    A. You will have a depressed mood (irritable for children and adolescents) nearly every day,

and/or

    B. You will take little interest or pleasure in your day-to-day life.

II. You will also be suffering from some of the following symptoms:

        – significant weight loss/gain (5% of body weight in 1 month) or appetite increase/decrease

        – insomnia/hypersomnia

        – observed psychomotor agitation/retardation

        – fatigue or loss of energy

        – feelings of worthlessness/guilt

        – decreased concentration/decision-making

        – thoughts of death/suicide

You will have had at least five of these symptoms for two weeks.

III. You will also need to be able to rule out other possible causes of your problem. You will need to rule out:

    A. organic illnesses such as heart disease, liver disease, stroke, etc. These diseases can make you look depressed when you are not.

    B. grief as a possible cause.

    C. other emotional illnesses which have some of the same symptoms, but also may be accompanied by hallucinations, delusions, or psychotic symptoms.

The danger here is that you might not admit you need help. You might keep the pain to yourself, like Andrea did for almost six years. Maybe you believe that you are ultimately responsible for how you feel. You tell yourself that you can snap out of it if you try hard enough. You think you can "will" yourself out of your depression, no matter how deep a depression it is.

The simple truth is that you cannot just "will" yourself free of depression. Recovery is not that easy. Unless you get help from someone, you will remain depressed, you will continue to suffer, and if your depression is serious enough, you may be at risk of attempting suicide. On the other hand, once you admit to yourself that you do need help, once you step through the doors of a psychiatrist's office, you will have taken the first of many steps down the road of recovery.

Dysthymic Disorder

If you suffer from dysthymia, you will have many of the same symptoms associated with major depression (see chart on page 60). You might eat too much and gain a great deal of weight, or you might not eat enough. You might sleep twenty hours a day or just four. You might lack energy and complain of feeling tired all the time. Or you might just be overwhelmed by a sense of helplessness. Dysthymic disorder is different from major depression in that the symptoms are not as severe. It is not as crippling or as pervasive as major depression, but it lasts longer. Dysthymic disorder does not prevent you from getting on with your life, but to do so takes greater effort. The problem with diagnosing someone as suffering from dysthymia is that the range of symptoms is just too broad, so the diagnosis tends to be just as broad and inconclusive.

If you suffer from dysthymic disorder, the chances are you will not face a depression as pronounced as major depression, but you will have to deal with it every day of your life. Dysthymia lasts for a long time—most of each day, most of the days in each week, and for at least two years. In some instances major depression can be superimposed on dysthymia, a condition known as "double depression."

Atypical Depression

Janie was blond, twenty-five, single, attractively dressed, with maybe a bit too much make-up. This was her fourth visit. She tried to stay calm and looked me squarely in the eye as we talked, but she was obviously upset. "I can't figure out what went wrong," she said.

DYSTHYMIC DEPRESSIVE EPISODES

I. If you are suffering from Dysthymic Disorder you will have the following profile:

    A. You will feel depressed for most of each day, for most of the days in each week, each month, and for at least two years.

    B. You will be suffering from at least two of the following symptoms:

        – poor appetite/overeating

        – insomnia/hypersomnia

        – low energy/fatigue

        – low self-esteem

        – poor concentration/difficulty making decisions

        – feelings of hopelessness

II. You will never be without symptoms for more than two months in a two-year period.

III. You will not have any of the following:

    A. any major depressive episodes in the first two years of the disorder.

    B. the symptoms of organic illnesses (heart disease, stroke, etc.).

    C. the symptoms of other emotional illnesses (delusions, manic episodes, psychotic episodes, etc.).

"What happened?" I asked.

"I don't know," she said. "That's just it. We went out a few times and everything was fine, and then last Friday we had a pretty big argument and I started to cry. I haven't seen him since."

"Do you want to see him?"

"I . . . I don't know."

Janie suffered from atypical depression. She did not have the classic—"typical"—symptoms of depression, but we both knew she was depressed. She had been depressed for quite some time.

Janie's "blue spells" began soon after she graduated from college. To begin with, she couldn't find a job she liked, that she could feel "a part of," as she put it. She often felt sad, even suicidal. Some days she wouldn't even get out of bed. It wasn't that she had trouble sleeping, she just didn't want to do anything.

She also felt nervous or anxious a lot of the time, though she couldn't say about what exactly, and so she started taking Valium on a regular basis. The Valium didn't work. Sometime later Janie told me that her mother had also suffered from feelings of anxiety, had also taken Valium for relief, but the Valium hadn't done much for her either.

Finally, Janie had a terrible time relating to other people, especially to men. She'd date someone for a while, and they'd do everything together, and then something would go wrong and that would be the end of the relationship. She told me she had gone from one relationship to another during the past few years and had yet to find any real satisfaction. Three days after her fourth visit, Janie overdosed and had to be hospitalized.

Not Just a Wastebasket Category

In a nutshell, atypical depression is any form of depression that is not typical. Admittedly, this sounds like we've made up a wastebasket category into which we can put all those patients who don't seem to fit into any other category. What we now call atypical we used to call neurotic. Yet the new classification is useful.

Let's say your doctor tells you you're atypically depressed. This means you suffer from a high degree of anxiety, unlike patients considered "typical." Your hands sweat. You often feel a queasiness in your stomach. Sometimes you can feel your heart beating rapidly. You also react to people and to situations with a great deal of emotion and often blame others for your own misfortunes. The difficulty Janie had relating to others illustrates this last point. Whenever she "broke up" with someone, she always blamed him for the breakup.

Patients who suffer from atypical depression really are different, and this is especially true when it comes to the kind of medication they will best respond to. They do not respond as readily to the conventional tricyclic antidepressants normally used in treating major depression.

Effective treatment of atypical depression will be a bit more difficult. There may be quite a few depressive disorders included in this single category. It may also take some time to determine which medication will be best. In Janie's case, it took about three months before we found the right medication and the right dosage. She is by no means "cured." There are no overnight miracles when it comes to treating depression. But she is much happier now, and much more confident. Last week she told me she'd been dating someone for close to four months. When I asked her if it was serious she just smiled.

Leaden Fatigue and Other Symptoms of Atypical Depression

A noted psychiatrist and researcher, Dr. Donald Klein, has developed some interesting criteria for distinguishing between some forms of atypical depression.[1] Klein focused his studies on thirty patients who failed to respond to tricyclic antidepressants, yet who responded favorably to monoamine oxidase inhibitors. He discovered that these patients fell into two main groups.

The patients of the first group displayed signs of major depression, yet they had a variety of "atypical" symptoms as well. These patients spent a great deal of time sleeping, were often tired, and suffered from a condition known as "leaden fatigue." They felt as if their arms and legs weighed a ton.

These same patients felt compelled to overeat and often gained a great deal of weight. They also exhibited what Klein calls a "chronic rejection sensitivity." They felt rejection anxiety even among their family and friends and would often anticipate such rejection by responding as if they had already been rejected.

Klein classified the second group under the term "hysterical dysphoria." The patients in this group seemed overly affected by applause and praise and were subject to sudden, and quite often extreme, mood swings. These patients were elated one moment and desperately unhappy the next. Their moods changed in response to what was going on around them. When they were in the lime-light, when they were admired by all, then they were able to function quite well. But when they felt rejected, they became very depressed. Some even began to talk about suicide.

Many of the patients who fell into this second group were women who reflected the very image of femininity which our culture promotes. They wore the right clothes, a little too much makeup, and their hair looked like it had been styled in the most expensive of hair salons. But in spite of how these women looked, they all had a difficult time dealing with other people, especially men, and often found themselves dealing with one "problem relationship" after another.

Klein's study was an attempt to distinguish between different types of atypical depression, first by observing the many different symptoms that each patient displayed, and second by classifying each patient according to the symptoms observed.

While the findings of this study may not point to any specific method for treating atypical depression, they do provide us with a key to understanding why some patients respond to one kind of medication and not to another.

Masked Depression

It was Saturday afternoon, a little after three. I had just come home from a picnic with my son and his family. The phone was ringing.

"Hello?"

"Herb? This is Eric. Do you have a minute?"

Eric was a good friend of mine, a pastor at one of the Baptist churches in town. He called because he was concerned about a member of his congregation and wanted to know if the three of us could meet in my office the next day. The man he spoke of was Martin.

Martin was in his early forties. He had a good family, a nice home, a responsible position with an insurance company, yet something was destroying the fabric of his life. For one thing, he had trouble sleeping at night and felt extremely tired as a result. He had also lost some weight. Martin believed these symptoms were the result of the problems he was having at work. He was under a lot of stress. The truth was, his problems at work were symptoms in themselves.

Martin's job called for him to make some pretty complicated decisions. He had always been quite good at his job, but he had been losing confidence in his own abilities of late and found that making even minor decisions was difficult, if not impossible. He began to put off making any decisions until the last possible moment, and when he finally made up his mind, he invariably felt he had made the wrong choice. He began to think he was in a job he wasn't qualified for, that all this time he had been fooling his bosses.

When I told Martin he was depressed, he shook his head and said he wasn't crazy. He couldn't see any relation between his problems and psychiatry, and he certainly didn't see how psychiatric treatment was going to help him. I talked with him about how being depressed is not the same as being crazy. I explained depression as an illness you can treat with medication, how you can be depressed and not even realize it. Martin agreed to go into treatment. Six weeks later, he felt a lot better, almost like his old self.

A Pain That Won't Go Away

Martin suffered from masked depression, a form of depression hidden behind a mask of apparent normalcy—at least to him. Neither he nor those he knew realized he was depressed because he seemed to be leading a normal life, struggling with the same kinds of problems we all struggle with. But underneath the surface, things were not normal. Martin was in a lot of pain, a pain that wouldn't go away.

If you suffer from masked depression, you do not show many of the classic signs of depression, you do not appear to be depressed, and yet you are depressed. The difference here is that your symptoms seem to be of a physical illness rather than of a mental illness.

Let's say you suffer from headaches. You take aspirin, you pull the shades and lie down, but nothing seems to work. Your headaches get worse and worse. You cannot function. To make matters worse, you don't realize the headaches are a symptom of depression, and so you might spend years going from one physician to the next in the hope of finding a cure. Unfortunately, no matter how many times you go to your doctor, no matter how many times you go to the hospital for tests or x-rays, your symptoms will inevitably return.

Most people suffering from masked depression believe their illness stems from something physical. This belief is a major stumbling block in effectively treating them. Most will respond to medication if you can get them to agree to take it. Unfortunately, not everyone agrees.

This was the case with John. I had known John and his wife, Evelyn, for a number of years, but I did not know the extent to which he and his family were suffering. When John went into the hospital for a series of diagnostic tests, Evelyn called me, and I found out just how serious things were. Evelyn told me John was undergoing these tests in the hope of discovering what was wrong with his stomach. He had been complaining for the past few months about a pain that came and went suddenly. He suffered from gas and diarrhea, and he said he felt bloated and incredibly weak. Evelyn was certain that his pain was not due to anything the doctors could find.

John had a history of such complaints. The first time he felt this way, almost twenty years earlier, he had his gall bladder removed. Since then, he had been in the hospital numerous times, only to have the doctors tell him they could find nothing wrong. But in spite of these past assurances, John was convinced that something was seriously wrong, and so he insisted that he go to the hospital for further tests. His physician was going to conduct an upper GI, a barium enema, and a colonoscopy, among other tests.

Though John was sure these tests would pinpoint his problem, Evelyn was not. Neither was I, so I asked Evelyn how John had been doing at home prior to his leaving for the hospital. She told me that he was irritable, tired all the time, and that he rarely took the time to join his family for dinner. She also told me that John was having trouble at work. John's family owned and operated a paper mill, and John was responsible for keeping track of shipments to current clients. Of late, he had begun to neglect this work, and some clients even called to complain that they had not received their orders. When I heard all this, I suspected that John was suffering from masked depression.

I wanted to start John on tricyclic antidepressants right away, but John wanted nothing of the kind. He told me he didn't need a psychiatrist to tell him how he felt. He said there was nothing wrong with his emotions and that was that. John has yet to seek psychiatric help. He is still going from physician to hospital to physician again in the hopes of finding a "cure." He is still depressed.

"Think" Depression

Many people like John refuse to seek treatment. And there are just as many people who never know they are in the midst of a depression. Some studies estimate that twenty to thirty percent of all the people who go to cardiac clinics have nothing wrong with their heart. This is also true for people who complain about pain of the gastro-intestinal tract. Most family practitioners see a good many people every year with symptoms that have more to do with depression than physical illness. These people come in complaining of just about everything: stomachaches, headaches, dizziness, heart palpitations, nausea, vomiting, back pain, vague abdominal pain, pain in the arms or legs or both. And even though their doctors can find nothing wrong with them, they continue to suffer from the same symptoms.

How can we help these people?

Let me answer that question by talking about my own experiences. I have received many calls over the years from physicians who have asked me to talk with people suffering from mysteriously recurring pains. This was how I met Tracy, a young housewife with two children. Tracy complained of a pain on one side of her face, a tingling, burning sensation on her right cheek, which also affected her tongue. She was very worried about this sensation, and after consulting with her personal physician, she checked herself into the hospital. The hospital staff ran numerous tests but could find nothing wrong with her.

When I saw Tracy, she looked depressed. She did not smile. She did not even look up. And she talked rather slowly. She told me that the burning sensation would not go away and that none of the doctors she had gone to seemed able to help. I spoke with her for over an hour. Had she been sleeping well? No. How about eating? Not too well either. And she had been losing weight for over a month. When I told Tracy she might be suffering from masked depression, she was visibly surprised. She had never considered the possibility that she might be depressed. Now, after three months of treatment, she is doing well.

Why wasn't Tracy's problem spotted earlier? Couldn't everyone see how much pain she was in? Well for one thing, most of the doctors she went to just weren't looking for depression. They were looking for some physical ailment. So was she. For another thing, even a psychiatrist may not recognize masked depression when he or she sees it because it doesn't look like depression. When I talked with Tracy, I was looking for signs of depression. Why? The answer is simple. If you hope to properly identify and treat depression, any kind of depression, you must be alert to its varying signs, even when they are hidden.

I don't mean to suggest that I find signs of depression in all of my patients, because I certainly don't. Not everyone who comes to see me is depressed. But I do "think" depression every time a patient walks through my door. And when patients complain of physical problems, I take them seriously. If I didn't, I might easily overlook the cause of someone's suffering.

6

From Great Pain to Great Joy, and Everything in Between

In the mid 1830s Charles Dickens became engaged to Catherine Hogarth, the daughter of a newspaper man. As always, he was the consummate egotist, thinking first of himself, and quite often only of himself. He loved to be the center of attention. One evening he dressed as a sailor and burst into the Hogarth household and began to dance a sailor's jig. When he finished dancing he disappeared out the front door, only to return moments later in a suit of his own, but thereafter he pretended to know nothing of the dancing sailor.

Manic Depression

In their book *The Key to Genius*, D. Jablow Hershman and Julian Lieb maintain that Charles Dickens was suffering from manic depressive illness and that the above incident reflects one of his more manic moments, for few but those in a manic state would be so creative, so energetic, so outrageous.[1] The life of Charles Dickens was filled with such moments.

After spending some time aboard a paddlewheel boat, Charles wrote the following in a letter:

It was blowing hard; and I was holding on to something—I don't know what. I think it was a pump—or a man—or the cow (brought for the milk) I can't say for certain, which. My stomach, with its contents, appeared to be in my forehead. I couldn't understand which was the sea and which the sky; and was endeavoring to form an opinion, or a thought, or to get some distant glimmering of anything approaching an idea, when I beheld standing before me, a small figure with a speaking trumpet. It waved, and fluctuated, and came and went, as if smoke were passing between it and me, but I knew by its very good-natured face that it was the captain. It waved its trumpet, moved its jaws, and evidently spoke very loud. I no more heard it than if it had been a dumb man, but I felt that it remonstrated with me for standing up to my knees in the water.—I was, in fact, doing so. Of course I don't know why. Sir, I tried to smile. Yes—Such is the affability of my disposition that even in that moment I tried to smile. Not being able to do so, and being perfectly sensible that the attempt faded into a sickly hiccough, I tried to speak—to jest—at all events to explain. But I could only get out 2 words. They bore reference to the kind of boots I wore, and were these—"Cork soles,"—perhaps a hundred times (for I couldn't stop; it was part of the disease)—The captain, seeing that I was quite childish, and for the time a maniac, had me taken below to my berth.[2]

For Charles Dickens, the exhilaration of mania was a way of life, and yet he also suffered through periods of depression. In August 1849 he suffered from a depression so severe he could scarcely function at all. Of himself he wrote to John Forster: "An extraordinary disposition to sleep (except at night, when his rest, in the event of his having any, is broken by incessant dreams) is always present; and, if he have anything to do requiring thought and attention, this overpowers him to such a degree that he can only do it in snatches: lying down on beds in fitful intervals. Extreme depression of mind, and a disposition to shed tears from morning to night, develops itself at the same period."[3]

During his manic periods, which were quite lengthy, Dickens accomplished a great deal, but because he also suffered from depression, he never accomplished as much as he had intended. As he grew older, his depressions became more frequent, he wrote less and less, and his physical health began to deteriorate. When he died in June of 1870 (he was only 58), he had not completed a major work in almost five years.

Peaks and Valleys

If you suffer from a manic depressive psychosis you bounce back and forth between two extremes. Your life is a cycle of ups and downs, peaks and valleys.

For a while you live in a state of mania, a condition marked by feelings of exaggerated intensity coupled with outbursts of tremendous physical and mental activity. There is no telling how long your mania will last. Some people live in such a state for weeks or months, others for only a matter of days.

After you "come down" from one of these manic highs, you may lead a relatively normal life for a while, a few months, maybe longer, but you will probably fall into a depression before the year is out. Again, there is no telling how long you will feel depressed. And when you do recover from your depression, the chances are that you will soon suffer from yet another manic episode.

This alternating between peaks and valleys is why we call manic depressive psychosis a bipolar disease, for it seems as if the patient is suffering from two diseases, not just one.

Who Needs Sleep?

When manic depressives enter a manic state, they are not just happy, they are in a state of euphoria. The condition is extreme to say the least. Manic patients seem to have an unlimited supply of energy, and many go for days with very little sleep. They move in quick and random succession from one thought to another, for their minds are overly active. They also speak with a great deal of speed, as if they have no control over the words that come literally pouring out of their mouths.

Many patients in the manic state have grandiose schemes about how they can change the world (like Napoleon) or how they can make millions of dollars. Others seem to take the opposite approach toward money and spend as much of it as they can. Some patients end up going through their bank accounts overnight. Most try to do too many things. Dickens would take on project after project when in a manic state. For those patients lost in the euphoria of mania, everything is possible.

In the most severe cases, manic depressive patients actually become psychotic. They tend to hallucinate—hearing voices, seeing things, talking to dead people and the like. When Dickens was immersed in the writing of a novel, he became convinced that his characters were alive, that they followed him around and talked to him. Many also suffer from delusions.

Rapid Cyclers and Dysphoric Manics

Patients who suffer from bipolar illness alternate between periods of manic behavior and periods of great depression, and the time it takes to experience both the high of mania and the low of depression is called a cycle.

Some patients go through a cycle only once or twice in a year, but others experience these cycles with a much greater frequency and may cycle four or more times in any one year. Such patients are known as rapid cyclers.

Other patients appear to be in the manic phase while at the same time suffering from signs of depression. They may feel great sadness, experience feelings of both hopelessness and helplessness, and they may even become suicidal. Such patients are known as "dysphoric manics."

MANIC EPISODES

I. If you are suffering from a manic episode you will have the following profile:

    A. You have an unrealistic sense of optimism (an elevated mood), though you may also be irritable.

and

    B. You will have at least three of the following symptoms:

        – an inflated sense of yourself

        – less need for sleep

        – pressured speech (talking so fast the words are a jumble)

        – racing thoughts (you will not be able to stop thinking)

        – a tendency to be easily distracted

        – an increase in goal-oriented activity

        – greater need to seek out pleasure in spite of possibly painful consequences

II. During a manic episode you will be unable to function normally in your job, at home, or with others.

III. You may need to be hospitalized to prevent your harming yourself or others.

IV. You need to rule out the following conditions:

    A. If you have delusions or hallucinations for as long as two weeks without mood symptoms.

    B. If the cause of your problem is organic (a physical ailment).

    C. If your mania is combined with another psychotic disorder.

One problem in treating patients who are "rapid cyclers" or "dysphoric manics" is that they do not respond as well to lithium. But the key to treating these patients is the same as it is for treating those who cycle only once or twice a year, whatever drugs are being used to treat them. Their symptoms need to be closely monitored, for as their symptoms change, as they move from one extreme to the other, their medication needs will change as well.

The Case of Robert

Robert was a tall man in his thirties, with a dark complexion, and he had been suffering from a manic depressive psychosis for almost three years. I had him on lithium in order to control his manic swings, yet I could see that he was still having problems. Robert was having trouble sleeping because he simply could not stop his thoughts from racing through his mind. Since this is a step toward mania, I put Robert on a drug called thorazine (in addition to the lithium). His sleeping patterns reversed themselves, and he was able to sleep once more.

When Robert entered the manic state, he exhibited a range of symptoms often associated with the most severe cases of this disease. He became delusional, paranoid, and overtly psychotic. The effects on his life were devastating. He lost his job as well as his family because he was unable to control his impulses during manic episodes. He emptied his bank account. His wife and children refused to have anything to do with him.

To make matters worse, Robert suffered from severe depression in between these manic episodes. During these depressive periods he withdrew completely from the world around him and rarely got out of bed. He had absolutely no energy.

Patients like Robert are difficult to treat. I can give them thorazine when they are in or near a manic state, but thorazine does them little good when they are depressed. I can give them antidepressants for their depression, yet I am well aware that by doing so I might send them into another attack of mania. The balance between mania and normalcy and depression is a delicate one. I must be alert to these symptoms, to even the slightest change in their mood, for they could easily develop into a full-blown mania.

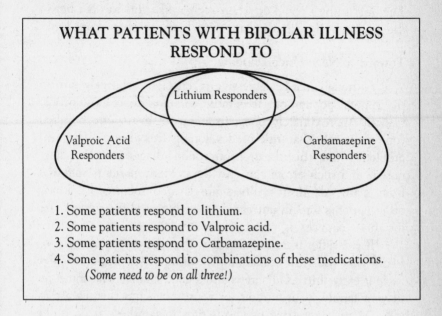

WHAT PATIENTS WITH BIPOLAR ILLNESS RESPOND TO

Lithium Responders

Valproic Acid Responders

Carbamazepine Responders

1. Some patients respond to lithium.
2. Some patients respond to Valproic acid.
3. Some patients respond to Carbamazepine.
4. Some patients respond to combinations of these medications.
   (*Some need to be on all three!*)

When Feeling "So Good" Is Not So Good

Pam was another patient suffering from this illness, though her symptoms differed dramatically. When Pam went into a manic state, she literally felt like she was on top of the world. She had a great deal of energy and thought herself capable of accomplishing anything. She felt so good, in fact, that she stopped taking her medication. But when Pam did this, she soon lost all control. Her mind began to race and she couldn't stop thinking. Then she began talking incessantly. She couldn't stop the words from pouring out of her mouth. Finally, she entered a state of euphoria.

When Pam reached this point, she resisted all my attempts to get her back on medication. She simply did not realize what was happening to her, that she was virtually self-destructing.

The only thing I could do when she got like this was put her in the hospital, though the last time I did so she escaped.

Toward a New Understanding

Although manic depressive psychosis is relatively rare in the general population, it is more common than most people realize. Approximately one person out of every one hundred (one percent) is at risk of developing this illness. The real problem is that this disease is often underdiagnosed or misdiagnosed, and such errors can cost lives. Many patients suffering from manic depressive illness are treated incorrectly. Many other patients remain untreated altogether, and the suicide rate for these patients is twenty-five percent.

If you suffer from this disorder, the chances are almost two to one that you are a woman, and most likely you began to suffer in your early thirties. There is also a good chance that someone in your family, your mother, or your uncle, has this disease as well. Manic depressive psychosis runs in families, as do other forms of depression.

The good news is that every day brings us one day closer to discovering the exact biological cause of this form of mental illness, and when we make this discovery, we will be able to treat it more effectively because we will know how to restore the exact biochemical balance that results in normal brain activity.

The Amish Studies

In a study of bipolar illness among the Amish population, an abnormal gene was linked to the development of manic depressive psychosis.[4] If these findings hold up, they will help to confirm yet again the general premise that certain forms of mental illness run in families.

The Amish themselves have been aware of this fact for many years. When they speak of this form of mental illness they say, "It is in the blood." They seem to realize that mental illness is not caused by stress, but by something "in the blood," something chemical.

The implications of this study are far-reaching. If one form of mental illness can be linked to an abnormal gene, as was the case in the Amish study, then perhaps it is only a matter of time before other forms of mental illness are linked to abnormal genes.

Cyclothymia

All of us have mood swings from time to time. Some days we feel good, other days we feel bad. Manic depressive mood swings are extreme to say the least. Cyclothymic mood swings are not so excessive. So what is cyclothymia? It may be a form of manic depression; it may be a separate illness. We do not really know. We do know that if you suffer from this disorder, your moods may change slowly, with relatively normal periods in between, or they may change more quickly. But again, we do not know why.

Those who suffer from cyclothymia have some of the same symptoms, though not as severe, as those patients suffering from manic depressive illnesses. When they become depressed, they may have problems sleeping. They may have less and less energy. In short, they go into what amounts to a social withdrawal. When they enter a hypo-manic state, their need for sleep decreases, but they also have a lot of energy. They may even have grandiose ideas or schemes and become impatient with those around them.

SYMPTOMS OF CYCLOTHYMIC DISORDER

I. If you suffer from cyclothymic disorder you will:

    A. have numerous hypomanic episodes and numerous periods of depressed mood or loss of interest or pleasure, which do not meet the criterion for major depression, during a two-year period (one year for children and adolescents).

    B. never be without symptoms for longer than two months during that two-year period.

II. If you suffer from cyclothymic disorder, there will not be:

    A. any clear evidence of a major depressive episode or a manic episode during the first two years (one year for children and adolescents) of disorder.

    B. any indication that your condition is part of any psychotic disorder.

    C. any evidence of an underlying physical (organic) cause.

Psychotic Depression

Her name was Marion. She was seventy years old and came to see me twice a month for almost two years. Marion believed that the police were coming to take her away because she stole a sweater from her next-door neighbor, a woman named Beatrice. She kept her bags packed just in case the police came to her door. She was extremely paranoid and believed that people have always been out to get her, that they watch her, talk about her behind her back, and call the police on her.

Marion suffered from psychotic depression, and her fears were but a symptom of her illness. She also lacked energy. She had a great deal of difficulty moving from her room in the nursing home to the lounge and so she spent most of each day in her room. She looked sad, felt sad, and acted sad. Worse still, she lived in a separate reality. Her thoughts and perceptions were distorted. From time to time she heard voices telling her that she was a bad person, that her life was hopeless. When she came to see me with her daughter, she often complained about how much each visit cost and how she would soon run out of money, even though there was no truth at all to what she said.

Life and Death Choices

People who suffer from psychotic depression tend to withdraw into a world of their own, a world separate from the problems and responsibilities of both work and family. While only ten percent of depressed patients suffer from this form of depression, the effects are most devastating.

Patients who are psychotic usually feel an overwhelming sense of futility. Life becomes meaningless. Many become deranged and suffer from hallucinations. Some may hear the voices of the dead, a brother who died in the last war, a mother who died in a car wreck, a friend who died of leukemia, voices beckoning them, urging them, telling them to kill themselves. How powerful are these voices? Patients suffering from psychotic depression have a higher rate of suicide than patients suffering from any other form of depression.

I first met with Marion because she had tried to kill herself. While visiting her daughter, she somehow got hold of a bottle of pills and swallowed every one. Her daughter brought her into the hospital at three o'clock on a Saturday afternoon. I saw Marion the next day.

Treating Psychotic Depression

The good news is patients who suffer from psychotic depression can be treated. Marion responded well to treatment. She hasn't had a suicidal episode like the one I described above for over a year. And though she is by no means "cured," she no longer seems to be a threat to herself.

The problem is that many times the psychotic features of

this disease are missed altogether. Hallucinations and delusions are not readily apparent.

Patients suffering from psychotic depression do not respond as well to antidepressants alone and need to be on neuroleptics as well. Electric convulsive therapy (see chapter 11) is also an effective means of treatment. But some patients, like Marion, need to be hospitalized for their own good, not only to help them recover, but also to keep them from doing themselves further harm.

Schizoaffective Disorder

Theresa, twenty-four years old, was in the emergency room of a downtown hospital. She had been running up and down the streets of her neighborhood at two in the morning, all the while yelling at the top of her lungs. Her neighbors called the police.

Theresa was tall and thin. She had long black hair, which hadn't been brushed in days. Her clothes were a mess. One look at her and you could see that she was completely out of touch with the world around her. She seemed to be suffering from schizophrenia, and yet she had manic symptoms as well.

According to her family, she had slept very little during the last few nights, yet she had a tremendous amount of energy. Her mind was very active and moved rapidly from one thought to the next. When she spoke her words literally tumbled out of her mouth (this is known as pressured speech). She said someone was after her. You could see the terror in her eyes. She said the voices kept talking to her, telling her that she couldn't get away, telling her that she might as well stop running. She said some of the voices had faces that were bloated and covered with warts. The voices followed her wherever she went. So did the faces.

We can safely say that Theresa was acutely psychotic, for she had a distorted view of reality. Theresa's psychosis was compounded by a variety of affective (mood) disorder symptoms. She showed a great deal of emotion in attempting to deal with her perceptions, even though her perceptions were distorted. This fact alone is an indication that she was probably suffering from schizoaffective disorder.

Schizophrenia

Schizophrenia is the most serious mental illness we deal with. It robs its victims of the potential of life itself. Many of our state hospitals and psychiatric clinics are filled with the victims of this disease.

In general, schizophrenia is a thought disorder, meaning that the most prominent feature of this illness is abnormal thinking. Schizophrenics become victims of a variety of delusions. They hear voices. They see things. Many believe they can read minds. Some claim to have received messages from outer space while watching TV. Some feel they are being controlled by some unknown force. Still others think that their brains are being eaten by worms. These patients are psychotic. They are out of touch with reality. And they exhibit little or none of the feelings by which most of us define what it means to be truly human.

Schizophrenia is *not* a form of depression. Often, however, patients with bipolar illness or schizoaffective disorder are misdiagnosed as suffering from schizophrenia.

Schizoaffective Disorder Is Not Schizophrenia

Schizoaffective disorder is an illness that is part schizophrenia and part affective disorder. (The word *affective* refers to a disorder marked by changes in the emotional state.) If you put manic depressive disorder (bipolar illness) on one end of a continuum, and schizophrenia on the other end, schizoaffective disorder would fall somewhere in between.

Schizoaffective patients are difficult to recognize and to diagnose, which makes getting the correct diagnosis all the more important. These patients are not manic depressive, but they do possess a variety of manic symptoms. Some have trouble sleeping. Some have an abundance of energy accompanied by grandiose schemes. Others may be depressed for a while, and then may become excited.

We used to think that anyone exhibiting signs of schizophrenia had schizophrenia. We now know that this assumption was wrong. Schizoaffective disorder is not schizophrenia, though here, too, they exhibit some of the same symptoms. Unfortunately, many patients with schizoaffective disorder are misdiagnosed as having schizophrenia and then are given the wrong medication. They continue to suffer, and that is a tragedy, for patients with schizoaffective disorder will respond when given the proper medication.

What We Know About Schizoaffective Disorder

We know that this disorder is a genetic-biochemical illness, but, as is the case with psychotic depression, there is a lot we don't know about it.

Schizoaffective disorder may be a separate illness, or it may be a number of illnesses linked together by similar symptoms. Some patients who seem to suffer from schizoaffective disorder may actually suffer from schizophrenia, while others may actually suffer from manic depression. We do know that this disorder is not as severe as schizophrenia, though in some cases patients become psychotic and need to be hospitalized.

We know that some patients diagnosed as schizoaffective respond quite well to lithium carbonate and when they are on this drug, they find themselves on the road to recovery. We also know that once we find the biochemical cause of this disorder, many others will find themselves on that very same road.

No Two Cases Are Absolutely Different

So far in this book, we have talked about depression as an individual kind of thing. Individuals become depressed, exhibiting a variety of symptoms, and then individuals are treated. No two cases are exactly alike. But the reverse is also true. No two cases are absolutely different either, for if this were so, then it would be virtually impossible to treat people for depression.

There are many similarities between one patient and the next. These similarities become all the more pronounced when we look at how depression affects whole groups of people. Women are two to three times more likely to become depressed than men. Children of all ages are suffering from depression, and some as young as six years old are committing suicide, or trying to. The elderly are often the most afflicted. If we want to do a better job treating people for depression, we need to see how depression affects these groups. In the next three chapters, then, we will look at how depression affects women, children, and the elderly.

— 7 —

Depression in Women

Most of my patients are women, depressed women, and if you take a look at the statistics, you would expect this to be the case. Women are twice as likely to suffer from major depression as are men. Women usually become depressed at an earlier age than do men. And women are also three times more likely to seek psychiatric help than men.

I don't mean to suggest that all women have exactly the same problems, for they don't, but women, as a group, have certain tendencies. Women experience a broad range of anxiety and mood disorders (premenstrual syndrome is part of this). Women may become extremely susceptible to alcohol and drug abuse. The good news is that all women can be treated. The bad news is that only twenty-five percent of all depressed women seek psychiatric help.

A Word About PMS

What is PMS? Is it related to depression? Is it another form of depression? What do we know about this condition? Well, we know that women experience significant hormonal changes, mainly in their estrogen and progesterone levels, during their periods. We know that during this time some women become angry or irritable. And we know that a good number become depressed, and some even become suicidal. Are all these women suffering from PMS? To be fair, I must admit that that's a trick question. The truth is that PMS is a kind of catch-all category for women who experience a similar, though not identical, set of symptoms.

One more thing about PMS. Since it can be so many different things, it is often tricky to treat. What works for one woman does not work for another. There are a wide range of treatment programs. Some psychiatrists prescribe progesterone to women with PMS, and for some this is helpful. Others prescribe any of a variety of drugs from standard antidepressants to some of the new generation antidepressants (like Prozac) to lithium. Some have tried giving their patients multivitamins. Others have even suggested surgery. Since PMS means different symptoms to different women, it is necessary to keep trying different programs until you find one that works for you.

A Jekyll and Hyde Story

Betsy was thirty-three, married, and she had two little boys ages five and two. She was sitting in my office because she suffered from PMS, and her case was severe.

"It used to start about three or four days before my period was due," she told me. "I'd become more irritable. I'd snap at my husband, at my kids. And for no real reason. One minute I'd be okay, and the next I'd be depressed, and I would stay depressed until I was into my period. I thought it was kind of normal, you know. I thought everyone went through the same thing, and I didn't really give it a lot of thought, except about eight or nine months ago it started getting worse."

Betsy stopped talking for a moment. She seemed a little unsure, a little unsteady. I nodded for her to continue, and she did.

"What I mean is I started becoming irritable six or seven

days before my period, not the three or four. And I was becoming even more irritable than I had been before. The smallest thing would set me off. I remember one evening after dinner I was washing the dishes and my husband came racing into the kitchen with the two boys racing after him. The next thing I knew I was screaming at the three of them and waving a spatula in the air."

Betsy was almost in tears at this point, and I asked her if she wanted to stop for a bit, but she smiled, shook her head, and then she continued.

"No, no. That's why I came to you. I don't know what to do. I don't know how my husband puts up with me, the poor guy. And the boys, they've become terrified of their mother. It's like I've become some sort of Jekyll and Hyde monster. I mean, everything's worse. I'm depressed more of the time. I'm more angry, more irritable. My whole personality has changed. And the worst of it is that it's now starting ten to twelve days before my period."

The scene that Betsy described is a scene that I have seen quite often. Many women who suffer from PMS find that their symptoms gradually become worse over time. Some of these women experience personality changes that affect their marriages, their families, their lives. Betsy was fortunate. She responded rather nicely to Prozac, which she now takes on a regular basis. She is no longer a Jekyll and Hyde type of monster. She no longer snaps at her husband. And her children are no longer afraid of her.

The Postpartum Blues

More than 2,400 years ago, Hippocrates suggested that women could become agitated, delirious, and suffer attacks of mania following childbirth. He was the first to define what we have come to know as the postpartum blues.

If you develop postpartum depression, you go through some dramatic changes both during and after childbirth. The most obvious of these changes is a shift in hormonal balance, which may cause feelings of great sadness, though the exact cause of this shift may be hard to pinpoint. Your psychiatrist may want to evaluate your thyroid, since the thyroid is sometimes the source of this imbalance. Whatever the cause, you will feel out-of-sorts to varying degrees. You may feel irritable and angry. You may have some trouble sleeping. You may wake up in the middle of the night and find you can't get back to sleep. You may also lose your appetite and find yourself losing weight. As we have seen with some other forms of depression, you may have no energy to get on with your life.

How serious are the "baby blues"? Many women, particularly young women, suffer from a mild form of postpartum depression after childbirth. In some cases, medication is needed, but most women soon recover. But one or two out of every ten women who suffer from the postpartum blues develop a severe depression. And one or two out of every thousand develop a psychosis. Women who suffer from such a psychosis suffer from hallucinations and delusions. They pose a very real threat to their lives, and to the lives of their children.

Before the Baby Is Born

Not all women wait until their baby is born before they become depressed. Some become sad and despondent already at the beginning of their pregnancy. Barbara was one such woman.

A few years earlier I had treated Barbara for a pregnancy-related depression. She was pregnant and depressed once again, and she had all of the typical signs: trouble sleeping, no appetite, no energy. During the first three months, I saw her twice a week, and I tried to help her see how important she was to her unborn baby, and to her entire family (this I call "supportive therapy"). I also met with her husband, her parents, and her brother to set up a support network to help them in the rough times ahead.

Once the first trimester was over, I started giving Barbara

medication, and she responded quite well, better than she had during her first pregnancy. She later delivered a fine baby daughter, and she was doing well herself, but I kept her on her medication and continued seeing her on a regular basis, because I knew that she was a prime candidate for depression.

A First-time Mother

Sarah had just given birth to a healthy, nine-pound baby boy. She was understandably exhausted, but she was also quite happy. Everything had gone according to plan. There had been no complications during the delivery. Her husband, Jack, had been with her the whole time. Her parents had ordered what seemed to be a truckload of flower arrangements to brighten up her hospital room. Two days later, she was on her way home.

For Sarah, trouble did not begin until the fourth day after her son had been born. She became listless. She could not sleep, except in fits. At three A.M. of the sixth day, her husband found her sitting in the middle of the baby's room, the baby asleep in her arms. She was crying uncontrollably.

Since Sarah had not planned to breast-feed her son, I put her on a tricyclic antidepressant. (If she had been breast-feeding, I would have kept her off of medication, unless her depression had been severe enough, in which case I would have urged her to stop breast-feeding.) Three weeks later, Sarah's crying had all but stopped.

The Baby in the Trash Can

One or two out of every thousand women who suffer from postpartum depression will develop a full-blown psychosis. These women will hallucinate. They will hear voices that may tell them their child is evil and needs to be killed. Many will begin to hate their babies. I hardly need to say that this condition is dangerous, or that these patients should be hospitalized and given emergency treatment. But all too often, no one recognizes this form of postpartum depression until it is too late. Every year young mothers kill their newborn babies. In some instances they even kill themselves.

I remember watching the news when they reported the case of a young girl, only fifteen, who gave birth to a baby in an alley across from her school. She put the newborn into a plastic garbage bag and stuffed the bag into a trash can. The man who found the baby said at first he thought it was a dead cat, but when he opened the bag, he saw there was a baby inside. The girl at first admitted what she had done, but later she claimed to have no memory of either the baby or the incident. The girl is currently undergoing psychiatric treatment.

Will I Get the "Baby Blues"?

We don't know for certain who will get the "baby blues" and who won't, but we can make some sound predictions based on statistical studies. If you have had a history of depression during your adolescence or early adulthood, or if anyone in your family (your mother, your father, your brother) has had a history of depression, then you are susceptible to postpartum depression. If you intend to have additional children, and you suffered from some form of depression after a previous birth, you have a twenty-five percent chance of developing postpartum depression once again.

The good news is that you can be helped through supportive therapy, medication, or a combination of both.

— 8 —

Depression in Children

We used to think that kids didn't get depressed. But no more. We are finding that many kids are depressed, even suicidal. They are, as far as diagnosis and treatment go, the new kids on the block. But because we are not used to the idea of depressed kids, we make two basic mistakes when treating them. We don't recognize the symptoms, and so we don't make the correct diagnosis. And when we do figure out that they are depressed, we don't administer the proper treatment.

Since severe depression is the same in children as it is in adults—meaning it is genetic and biochemical—we must treat depressed children with medication. Once, many child psychiatrists were reluctant to do this. Now, with the rapid development of psychopharmacology (the use of drugs in treatment) in child psychiatry, this attitude is changing. Child psychiatrists are beginning to realize the value, even the necessity, of using medication in treating the young.

Depression in Young Children

Mark seemed like any other eight-year-old kid when I first met him. He was wearing what he called a surfer's shirt along

95

with a pair of shorts and black high-tops—high fashion for a young boy. He was very bright and was doing well in school. Mark had a particular talent for computers. He also got along well with his mother. The two of them were joking around and laughing as they entered my office. So why was Mark's mother concerned? Why was Mark coming to see me? The simple truth was that Mark was depressed.

Mark's mother told me that Mark had become more and more irritable over the last few months. He would get angry a lot, and over trivial matters. Sometimes he would even hit himself. His behavior struck Mark's mother as abnormal, especially since it often arose for no apparent reason. What really scared his mother was when Mark would say that he didn't want to be alive. At first she thought Mark was going through a phase, like any other little boy, but when this phase continued, she took Mark to a psychologist, who referred him to me.

Mark and I talked about what bothered him, about why he got angry and lashed out. Mark said it was a lot of little things, but nothing in particular. His sister got on his nerves most of the time (somewhat typical of an eight-year-old boy) or he didn't get his way. Mark said that sometimes it got so bad he just wanted to be gone.

In talking with Mark, I soon realized that he was severely depressed. His frustration, anger, and talk about suicide were symptoms. I learned that Mark didn't have many friends at school and would just as soon play with his computer as with kids his own age. I also learned that Mark's family had a history of depression.

I must point out that Mark came from a good family. All too often we associate depression with troubled families, but this is not necessarily the case. Mark's parents were young, well-educated, and happily married. His home was a warm and responsive environment. But Mark's mother and his grandmother had both suffered from depression at one time during their lives, and so Mark himself was a prime candidate for depression.

Fortunately, Mark responded to medication and therapy (as did his mother). I knew he was making good progress when his mother told me he had spent the night at a friend's house.

Are Your Children At Risk?

If you have suffered from major depression some time during your life, there is a good chance that one or more of your children will too. The same is true if someone in your family has suffered from manic depression illness or alcoholism.

In a study conducted at Yale in September of 1984, researchers determined that the risk of depression in children ages six to seventeen increased dramatically in children whose parents were also depressed as opposed to children whose parents were not.[1] For those children whose parents suffered from depression as well as some other disorder (anxiety, panic attacks, etc.) the risk was even greater.

How Do You Know If a Child Is Depressed?

Many people ask me what I see in kids that makes me think they are depressed. There are a variety of indications.

Sometimes the youngsters just come right out and tell me. Many times they are visibly unhappy. Some of them have trouble sleeping. Either they can't fall asleep, or they wake up at odd times during the night, and they often complain of being tired all the time.

Some kids blame themselves for every little thing that goes wrong in their lives, no matter what the real cause. Some withdraw into themselves. They stop spending time with their friends. They seem to respond to the world in slow motion. They move slowly. They act slowly. They even think slowly. These kids just can't seem to motivate themselves. One sign of this may be falling grades.

Other kids become extremely agitated. They can't sit

quietly. They are irritable, argumentative, and even antagonistic. Still others display major personality changes, happy and outgoing one minute, withdrawn and paranoid the next.

Finally, some children become morbidly preoccupied with death and dying. Such symptoms are a strong indication of depression and should not be ignored. This is especially true in cases in which the child contemplates suicide.

Depression in Teenagers

As children enter their teenage years, they are more likely to suffer from depression than when they were younger. In a study of teenage students (ages fourteen to sixteen), researchers found that eight percent suffered from major depression or dysthymic disorder, which is twice the level for pre-adolescent children. Other studies have determined that the risk of major depression actually triples as children move from childhood to adolescence.

Depression is a fact of life for many teens. And, as we saw with depression in pre-adolescents, depression in adolescents is often misdiagnosed. Even when it is identified correctly, it is often improperly treated. Treating adolescents with depression is no different than treating anyone else with depression. But if we fail to recognize that adolescents can indeed suffer from depression, we won't be able to help them.

Symptoms in Depressed Adolescents

I have found that many of the same symptoms present in young children suffering from depression are also present in depressed adolescents. Children who were once friendly become sullen and withdrawn. They find they are unable to concentrate on their schoolwork and so their grades fall. They may have trouble sleeping through the night. They may become irritable or angry, often arguing for no apparent reason. They may begin taking drugs or become sexually active. And finally, in the most severe cases, they may become preoccupied with death, with dying, and with suicide.

It Can Happen to the Brightest

Barbara was a popular seventeen-year-old in one of the largest high schools in the city. She maintained a straight-A average and was the editor of the school yearbook. Evenings she helped her mother around the house. Weekends she relaxed with her boyfriend, someone she had known for almost five years.

Barbara seemed to have every aspect of her life under control. She seemed to lead the kind of life we all wish for our children. And yet Barbara told her mom and dad that she thought she was depressed, that she just knew she was. She told them she had been feeling sad a lot of the time and that she found it too difficult to concentrate on her school work. She didn't know what to do. Her mom and dad sent her to me.

The first thing Barbara told me was that she had been going through violent mood swings. One minute she'd be happy, feeling fine, then a few minutes later she'd get angry at something or at someone, like she was about to explode, and a few minutes after that she'd fall into a depression.

Barbara was concerned because these mood swings were happening with greater and greater frequency. She also told me that she had been having a really hard time getting to sleep at night, and that she had been suffering from some rather painful headaches. Then we talked a little bit about her feelings.

"I'm in the top three or four of my class," she said. "I'm really beginning to feel the pressure. I guess that's part of why I'm so depressed. I've lost my ability to concentrate. All I do in the afternoons is sleep. And if I think about what I should be doing with my life I start to cry. Some of the time it gets so bad that I don't want to be around anyone, not my family, not even my friends. I get angry and frustrated, and all I want is to be left alone."

When we think of depression, whether in adults or in children, we do not immediately think of people like Barbara. Barbara is a bright young lady, hardly rebellious, and she comes from a good family, a "together" family, and yet she is depressed. Why is this so? What accounts for depression in normally vibrant young people? I think most of the reason lies in the fact that Barbara's family, in spite of their togetherness, has had a history of depression. Barbara's uncle was an alcoholic, and both her mother and her older cousin had once suffered from severe depression. Barbara responded to medication. Her depression lifted, and she was her old self again.

Sometimes Medication Is Not Enough

There are many kids, like Barbara, for whom medication, along with supportive therapy, can do the trick. There are just as many who need counseling as well as the proper medication. They need to talk to someone who understands what they are going through, someone they can trust, but finding such a person is rarely easy.

Many of these kids come from broken homes. Mom is trying to hold down a job and be both mother and father to her children, and she just doesn't have the time to give to her teenage daughter or son. And so these kids feel ignored. They often think that nobody really cares about what happens to them, particularly their parents, so they try to face the problems of life on their own. They are often overwhelmed.

Take the case of Sally. She was only fourteen, and yet she was in the emergency room of a local hospital because she had cut her wrist. The wound was not deep. None of her tendons, muscles, or nerves were severed; but the fact that she had taken a knife to her wrist was a sign that she could be suffering from depression. Was Sally trying to commit suicide? I cannot say. What I can say is that her actions were a cry for help, a cry for someone to talk to. That someone happened to be me.

I talked with Sally for two hours, and persuaded her that

she needed to be in a hospital. She was a little reluctant at first, but I think she was also relieved that someone had taken the time to talk about what would be best for her. She stayed in the hospital ten days, during which time she started on medication. She also took part in group and individual therapy. In Sally's case, hospitalization and therapy helped. Her depression lifted.

A Case of Determined Resistance

Not every teenager wants to be helped. Some resent their parents, and so they end up resenting anyone their parents send them to for help. They reject any kind of medication and therapy. Many do not even realize how seriously ill they are.

Cathy was such a teenager. At sixteen she was quite a sight, like something out of a B-grade horror film. She wore black lipstick, black and purple fingernail polish, and black eye shadow. Her hair was mostly black as well, though streaked with brown and blond, long in the back and spiked on top. Her clothes were also black—jeans and a T-shirt. Cathy was not happy to be in my office. Her eyes focused on the floor, both sullen and withdrawn.

"She's either in her room or out with her friends," her mother said. "She doesn't much like helping out around the house. And when I try to talk to her about staying home once in a while, she just gets angry. She doesn't get along with anyone. Not me. Not her father. Not even her little brother."

I just listened to Cathy for a while. She didn't want to see me or talk to me at all, but her parents forced her to come, so there she was. She didn't understand why her parents were so strict with her. They didn't like her friends, and they didn't like her hanging out at the mall with them. They didn't like it when she came in at 12:30 or 1:00 in the morning. And they didn't like the way she dressed.

Then Cathy began to vent her frustrations.

"I don't know what their problem is," Cathy said. "I just

want to be left alone. I just want to live my life the way I want to."

I felt the anger of Cathy's words.

"I guess I have trouble falling asleep at night," she said. "That's why I stay up to two or three. Then I have to get up in the morning. My mom makes me. I'm tired the rest of the day. Every day. Sometimes I just wish I wasn't around. Then nobody'd have to bother."

Cathy admitted to me that she felt sad and depressed a lot of the time. She told me that one of her friends had tried to cut her wrist and had to be taken to the hospital. Cathy said the whole thing really shook her up, that her friend was now in a psych ward and that whenever she thought about her friend, she got real sad. She also told me that she spent a lot of time in her room, listening to records or tapes, or just sitting on her bed.

"My family's not much fun to be with," she says. "They just don't understand me. They don't even try."

Cathy looked depressed, and she sounded depressed. She also came from a family with a history of depression. When I spoke with her I was convinced she would be helped by medication and therapy, but she wanted neither. Cathy didn't even show up for her next appointment.

A Reason For Optimism

Fortunately, not all teenagers suffering from depression are like Cathy. Most are willing to talk about what's bothering them. Most are willing to take medication. More and more psychiatrists understand that adolescents can become depressed as easily as anyone else. This means that more and more teenagers are being properly diagnosed and properly treated. And more and more, they are rediscovering the joy of what it means to be young.

— 9 —

Depression in the Elderly

All of us will grow old. As we do, we will lose some of our capacity to think clearly, to reason, to remember. In extreme cases, this condition is known as senile dementia (or Alzheimer's disease), and is often linked to depression in the elderly, in most cases making their depression even worse. But not everyone suffering from memory loss and disorientation is suffering from dementia. Many are actually suffering from depression.

When older people become depressed, they often become deluded, believing in things that have no basis in reality. Many become paranoid, thinking that everyone is out to get them, that they have little or no money, that they will have nowhere to live, nowhere to go. It doesn't matter whether their fears are justified, for many are not. Fear becomes the order of the day. Depression becomes a way of life. And while many of these people have been depressed off and on throughout their lives, for many others, the experience is brand new.

The Case of Mrs. Wright

Mrs. Wright was seventy-nine years old. She was in my office because her daughter was concerned about her mental state. The daughter told me that her mother was having problems with her memory, that she got confused, couldn't find things, forgot where she had planned to go, and didn't seem able to cope with the routine of living anymore. She told me that her mother was also becoming more and more irritable and demanding.

Mrs. Wright said she didn't know what was going on. She thought she was running out of money (a common enough fear among the elderly), and she didn't know what to do about it. She had to pay her doctors and take care of her house, and she just didn't know how she was going to make it. She also said her children were all against her and that they kept talking about putting her in some kind of a nursing home. She most certainly did not want to go to a nursing home.

"Is it any wonder I can't sleep at night?" she asked me. "What with all these thoughts going around and around in my brain. Is it any wonder at all?"

Mrs. Wright was suffering from depression.

The first thing I did in treating Mrs. Wright was review the medication she had been taking. In many cases, elderly patients are over-medicated. The best medicine for such patients is no medicine, at least at first; otherwise there's no telling what the real problem is.

Mrs. Wright had been on four different drugs during the last year, and she was currently taking Xanax. I immediately took her off all medication for two weeks to give her body a chance to recover from the medication, and to give me a chance to see how depressed she really was. A good many of my older patients brighten up considerably once they're off their medication, and they begin doing things they haven't done in years. One woman, close to seventy, actually started dancing in my office one week after she had stopped taking her drugs. Of course

I do keep a close eye on the progress of such patients, and if I find that they need medication as an essential part of their treatment, then I will put them back on it.

Then Mrs. Wright had a physical exam, and I put her through a series of laboratory tests. Many elderly people suffer from heart disease, or from kidney or liver problems, though this was not the case with Mrs. Wright. But in some cases, what is first perceived as depression is in fact a reaction to a physical illness. In other cases, these illnesses intensify a depression that already exists, making treatment more complicated. Finally, some elderly patients exhibit the symptoms of depression because they don't eat the right foods or drink enough fluids. All these patients need is to adjust their diet. They need to eat regularly and drink more fluids.

Mrs. Wright's exam and lab tests indicated nothing unusual, so I put her on medication. After a few months of treatment she seemed much better. She was no longer so confused. She was no longer so irritable or demanding. She and her daughter even went out to lunch, and for once, they didn't argue about money.

Is It Alzheimer's, or Isn't It?

Several years ago I saw a patient who had been diagnosed by doctors at a top medical school neurology clinic as suffering from Alzheimer's disease. She had the typical signs—memory loss, confusion, and disorientation. But in many cases, the symptoms of Alzheimer's and those of depression are indistinguishable, and for this reason, depression is often missed when Alzheimer's is present.

When I saw this woman, I immediately thought depression. She said she had a hard time sleeping through the night. She rarely felt like eating and had lost a lot of weight over the past few months. And she said she felt that her life was an unending series of dreary days. She had absolutely no energy.

I started her on antidepressants, and her outlook on life

turned around 180 degrees. She no longer had problems sleeping. Her appetite improved. And she got some of her energy back. This sort of recovery doesn't happen all the time, but it does happen.

A Final Word on Treating the Elderly

When I treat elderly patients, I watch them closely, to see how they react to their medication. I also talk to them as well as to members of their families on a regular basis, sometimes every week. In many cases, I have found that supportive psychotherapy can help elderly patients and their families cope with the pain of depression.

Treating elderly patients can become quite complicated. Like many other depressed patients, elderly patients need someone they can rely on, someone who will listen to them. But the families of elderly patients also need someone they can rely on, someone who can help them care for older family members when those members can no longer care for themselves.

Some families just do not have the energy or the time to take care of their parents. And though nobody likes to send a parent, someone once strong-willed and independent, to a nursing home or a supervised apartment, sometimes there is no other choice. Many families feel a great deal of guilt after they have committed one or more parents to such a place.

The only thing that I, as a psychiatrist, can do in such circumstances is to lend a shoulder to cry on and a listening ear. I try to be both helpful and supportive when dealing with the families of elderly patients. This is sometimes the best medicine.

10

From Grief to Suicide

In 1849, the English poet Thomas Lovell Beddoes committed suicide. He had been a poet of only sporadic output, largely because of his own insecurities, and as he grew older he became more and more despondent over his lack of success, and more and more obsessed with the thought of his inevitable death. Was he depressed? Certainly. Was he overcome with grief, with sadness? This seems likely too. But perhaps the words of this poet describe best how he felt:

> If thou wilt ease thine heart
> Of love and all its smart,
>> Then sleep, dear, sleep;
> And not a sorrow
>> Hang any tear on your eyelashes;
>
> But wilt thou cure thine heart
> Of love and all its smart,
>> Then die, dear, die;
> Tis deeper, sweeter,
> Than on a rose bank to lie dreaming
>> With folded eye.

What happened to Thomas Lovell Beddoes almost 150 years ago still happens to people today, and illustrates how grief and sorrow can become depression (Beddoes would have called this feeling melancholy). Depression can lead to suicide. Of course, not everyone who feels grief, or sorrow, or sadness, or pain, becomes depressed. And not everyone who becomes depressed commits suicide, or even contemplates such action. But there is a distinct connection between grief and depression, and between depression and suicide.

When Grief Is Normal, and When It Isn't

You've probably experienced grief at one time or other in your life. Grief is universal. You would certainly grieve if someone you loved died—your mother or father, one of your brothers or sisters, your spouse or any one of your children. You might also grieve for any number of other reasons. Perhaps you lost your job and now find yourself in desperate financial straits. Perhaps you are recently divorced or separated. Perhaps your kids do not get along with each other. Your grief is a normal, healthy, though certainly temporary, response to all of these situations, and to many more besides. Feelings of grief are a necessary part of coping with life's trials. Grief is part of the process of living.

The chances are you will eventually recover from your grief, even though this may take up to several months. This, too, is normal. But there are times when grief is no longer healthy, no longer normal. If you grieve for longer than you should, for longer than is reasonable, if you find you are no longer able to take care of your responsibilities both at work and at home, then you need to seek help, for your grief has become depression.

Exactly when and how grief turns into depression I do not know. The symptoms of both are similar, so the distinction between the two is often blurred. Some of my patients who are suffering from prolonged grief have been depressed before.

Others have family members with a history of depression. But when they begin to show the classic symptoms of depression, when they have problems sleeping at night, maintaining their weight, enjoying their work, when they have problems just plain living their lives, then I am sure their grief has become depression.

Two Case Studies

Two of my patients suffered from depression caused by extreme grief. Both were middle-aged women. Both had recently lost children.

The first woman, Linda, lost her sixteen-year-old daughter in a car accident. Linda and her husband were both Christians. They were committed to Christ, involved in their church, and had even gone to Cuba to do relief work. But they just didn't understand why their daughter, Lisa, had to die. Lisa was a top student; she was popular, athletic, a member of Young Life, and a good kid all the way around. She and two of her friends were driving home from a late movie when a drunken driver slammed into the side of their car. Lisa was killed instantly. Her friends survived.

When Linda came to see me, the first thing she asked was how God could take her little girl like this. She was inconsolably upset and spent most of her time crying. She told me she had trouble both sleeping and eating. Linda seemed to have given up on life. She was severely depressed, which is why I put her on antidepressants immediately.

The second woman, Joan, lost her only daughter in another car accident. She also was an active Christian, but over the course of a year her faith had been sorely tested. She spent a lot of her time crying and moping aimlessly about her house. She was so unhappy, so depressed, that she was unable to get a full night's sleep for almost ten months. I put her on antidepressants as well.

Both of these women suffered profound losses which they

will carry with them for the rest of their lives. In the process of dealing with those losses, they each developed severe depressions. I am truly thankful they were both Christians because I believe the Lord can provide a great deal of comfort in situations involving the death of a child. I am also thankful they took the medication I prescribed because if they hadn't, they would be suffering even more than they are.

If you, like either Linda or Joan, are suffering from a major loss, the death of a child, a parent, or any other loved one, you are at risk of developing a severe depression. Unfortunately, if you become so depressed, your depression may go undiagnosed and untreated simply because most people will assume that your grief is temporary, that it will fade at some point, and that when it does fade, you will be able to get on with your life.

The sad truth is that major depression in grieving people is often missed, and so these people are left to "work through" their grief all on their own.

To Be or Not to Be?

In Shakespeare's *Hamlet*, the title character, Prince Hamlet, considers suicide as a way out of his problems. Why did Hamlet think about killing himself? What was going on in his life that led him to such thoughts? What was his emotional state of mind?

Hamlet's circumstances were certainly grim. His father was dead, murdered by his uncle, who had then married his mother. Instead of responding in anger and revenge, however, Hamlet fell into a deep depression. One of the characters, Polonius, explains how Hamlet

> Fell into a sadness, then into a fast,
> Thence to a watch, thence into a weakness,
> Thence to a lightness, and, by this declension,
> Into the madness wherein he now raves.

By the middle of the play, Hamlet's depression leads him to the brink of suicide. In his famous soliloquy, Hamlet wonders which is more important, "to be, or not to be." In this, too, Shakespeare demonstrates just how much he knew about human psychology. In some cases, depression really does lead to suicide.

Billy: On the Brink of Suicide

When I get into the classroom I sit down, but I don't bother with even a pen. I know I'm going to flunk this test, so why bother? All I do is sit there. I don't even read the questions. Who has time to read? Besides, there's too much going around in my head. I can't even focus on the questions. There's just too many thoughts.

I heard there's something happening out at the beach tonight. Lots of beer. Lots of women. Maybe I'll give Steve a ring and we can check it out. It could be a good time. And then I ask myself: Why won't Jennifer talk to me anymore? What did I do wrong? All I wanted to do is talk with her. Just for a few minutes. And then I look at my test again. What am I doing here? I'm no student. Anyway, who cares about the Spanish/American War? I'm too stupid. What made me think any different?

When the bell rings, the other students hand in their tests. I hand in mine too. Then I walk out of the room. I know I flunked the test, but I tell myself it doesn't matter. Hey! I didn't even put my name on it. I laugh. Maybe he won't know it's mine. Then I head into the parking lot, get into my car, and I drive away.

I don't know how long I drive around. Two or three hours. I don't care. I think about going home for supper, but I don't feel like dealing with my dad so I don't go. He's got this hang-up about me driving around like I do. He says I'm nothing but a crud. He says I'm going nowhere. I tell him nowhere is as good a place as any other, but he doesn't listen to me.

All of a sudden I am filled with shame and a deep sadness. What am I doing here? What's happening to me? I don't need this. Do I? Why don't I just go home? I don't understand what's come over me, but in a few minutes I am crying uncontrollably. It gets so bad I can hardly make out the road, so I pull into the parking lot of this public park and I get out of the car.

I don't know what time it is, but it seems pretty late. The park is deserted, which is good, because I feel bad enough without having to face any people. I lean back against the side of the car for a while, look up at the sky, at the stars. When I stop crying, I start walking, but I don't get very far. I stop in the middle of a tennis court and sit down by the net.

Although I am no longer crying, I still feel sad, but there's nothing I can do about it. Nothing anybody can do. Not really. And then I remember about the Spanish/American War and how all the people who fought in it are dead now. Dead people from a dead time. I imagine myself a part of the war. I close my eyes and I imagine myself in the heat of the action, a gun in my hand. And then the battle is over and I see a soldier lying in a field and he is dead.

I find this image strangely compelling, though at first I am not sure why. And then I know why. The face I see is completely at peace. No worries. No pain. No frustrations. No tears. I look a little closer, and I see that the soldier is me. The face is mine. For a moment I can think of nothing but how wonderful death must be. To find such peace. To find such freedom.

Then I open my eyes and I see that it is morning. I have spent the night sitting in the middle of a tennis court. And even though I am still thinking about the peace of death, I get up from the court, walk to my car, and go to school.

A Little Background

Billy was eighteen years old and a senior in high school. He couldn't say exactly when he began suffering from depression, but he admitted that it had been with him ever since grade school.

"It's not that I've been unhappy my whole life," Billy told me during our first meeting. "But I've always had some trouble learning to handle my emotions, especially in new situations."

When Billy started the third grade, he and his family had

just moved to the area. He was the new kid in school. He never really enjoyed school, and to be the new kid, the one without any friends, made life twice as hard.

"On the first day of school I didn't say a single word," he told me. "My teacher tried to get me to open up, but that only made me more frightened. By the middle of the day I was cowering in the corner of the lunch room. I wasn't going to move. I don't really know why I reacted like I did. The only thing I remember is this paralyzing fear that just took over. I wasn't going to move from the corner because I was afraid to."

When the school called Billy's mother, she came and took him home. It was then that the trouble between Billy and his dad started up. His dad said that Billy had everybody else fooled, but not him.

"Dad said I was just trying to get out of my schooling like any normal boy. He said he wasn't going to let me get away with it, that I was going to learn the way I was supposed to, and so back I went the very next day."

Eventually Billy settled down, but he didn't do very well that year. Every now and then he had those feelings again, just like on that first day, and his mother would come and take him home. By the time he was in junior high school, his list of symptoms had grown. He had become more frustrated, angry, and irritable. He would blow up for the most idiotic reasons.

"I'd be walking down the hall to my homeroom," he said, "books in hand. I'd drop one, but instead of bending down to pick it up, I'd get mad and start kicking it down the hall. The more I kicked it, the madder I got. My classmates thought I was crazy, so most of them left me alone."

When Billy entered high school, he had only two friends. Though they tried to help him through school, they weren't able to make things any easier for him. Every year was tougher than the one before. Billy also started having trouble sleeping, and that's when he started driving aimlessly around town in his car.

By the middle of his senior year, Billy had given up on school and on himself.

"I wondered why life seemed to be so difficult," he told me. "I thought maybe God had something to do with it. Like he was trying to tell me that I wasn't going to make it no matter how hard I tried, like maybe the best thing was for me to give up. That's when I started to think seriously about suicide. I guess I thought I had no other choice."

A Better Way

Billy came to see me when his school's psychologist urged him to do so. We talked for an hour about what his life was like, how much trouble he had been having both at home and at school, and after a while, Billy began to realize that he had been suffering from depression for years. I told him that he needed to be on medication if he wanted to feel better about himself. By the end of that first session Billy agreed to give my suggestion a try. I put him on imipramine.

Within five months, Billy's life turned around dramatically. He hasn't had a suicidal episode since he began taking his medication. He started doing things with his family, going to church and out to eat. He still argued with his dad, but the arguments were not as violent as they once were. He even began to show a greater interest in school and seemed determined to graduate.

The last time Billy came to see me we talked about what the future held. He said he wanted to go to college and study medicine. He said he wanted to be a psychiatrist. If I had to make one prediction about his life, I would say that he's going to make it.

Who Commits Suicide? And Why?

The overall suicide rate in the United States is twelve for every 100,000 deaths. This may not sound like such a high number, but those numbers add up. Every year, 29,000

Americans take their own lives. (Suicide is the eighth leading cause of death in the U.S.) And each number represents a person who was in trouble, a person who needed help, a person who saw no other alternative but to commit suicide.

Who are these people, and why do they commit suicide? There are a number of statistical factors we can consider.

First, more males commit suicide than females. Three men commit suicide for every woman. Suicide rates are lower for women in all age groups. However, more women attempt suicide than men. Men use more lethal means and therefore succeed more often at committing suicide.

Second, the older people get, the more likely they are to commit suicide. Most suicide victims are ages fifty and older.

Third, more white males commit suicide than non-white males.

Fourth, more single people commit suicide than married people.

Fifth, people suffering from alcoholism have a much greater chance of committing suicide than those without this disease.

And sixth, people with psychiatric problems (schizophrenia, agoraphobia, depression, to name a few) are much more likely to commit suicide than people without such problems.

What to Watch Out For

Symptoms. What symptoms do potentially suicidal people exhibit? Are these symptoms universally recognized? Unfortunately, anticipating or predicting suicide based on symptoms is difficult. Most symptoms do not clearly reveal suicidal potential. Even so, predicting suicidal behavior is not altogether impossible. Dr. Bech has shown that a feeling of hopelessness accompanies suicidal behavior more than any other symptom. Despair seems to be a more telling factor than even the severity of depression.

The Role of Life Events. In many cases, a tragic experience, a series of failures, or some other horrible event precedes suicide. For older patients, the death of a spouse or loved one quite often triggers suicidal thoughts. Oddly, divorce or forced separation does not seem to have the same effect.

The Timing of Suicide. When people suffering from psychiatric illnesses commit suicide, they usually do so early on, either during the beginning stages of their illnesses, or shortly after their treatment has begun. This is especially true for depressed patients. In one study, ten percent of depressed patients who committed suicide did so while still in the hospital, and fifty percent committed suicide within six months of being discharged.[1]

Again and Again and Again

As a group, most of the people who commit suicide are single, unemployed males in their thirties or forties. Many are suffering from either depression or schizophrenia. Many have previously attempted suicide as well. And yet there are many more people who attempt suicide time and again and do not succeed in ending their lives.

One young woman I know named Karen tried a dozen times to kill herself. I first met her after her tenth attempt. One of her roommates had brought her to the emergency room of a university hospital where she had her stomach pumped. Karen had apparently taken an entire bottle of aspirin and then a bottle of wine. When she woke up the next morning she said she was going to try again, and three weeks later, she did. The last I heard, she was being treated for depression.

Most of the people who, like Karen, are unsuccessful in their attempts to commit suicide are single, unemployed women under the age of thirty. They also suffer from depression. In most cases, they usually try to kill themselves by taking sleeping pills, or something similar. In contrast, those who successfully commit suicide usually use more lethal means—shooting themselves, hanging themselves, or jumping from a great height.

Teenage Suicide

Eight years ago the daughter of a very good friend committed suicide. Her name was Claire, and she was only fourteen. Attractive, popular, and a good student, she was an only child. She was also depressed. One afternoon she came home from school, found her dad's gun, and shot herself. I can hardly believe she is gone even now. Her death was a tragedy, a mind-numbing tragedy.

I went to her school along with her pastor to speak with her classmates. I remember standing on the podium and looking down upon the many faces, and all I could think was what a waste, what an awful tragedy. I hardly knew then what to say to those children gathered in that auditorium. I would not have the same problem now.

I would talk with them about their feelings of grief and loss, about how to cope with these feelings, but I would also tell them that Claire's death was preventable. I would tell them that every teenager who thinks about suicide is also depressed, and then I would explain that we could prevent all teenagers from committing suicide if we could just treat them for depression. We are beginning to recognize which teenagers might harm themselves, and why they might do so. We are beginning to put the pieces of the teenage suicide puzzle together.

What Teenagers Are at Risk?

Are there some kids who have a greater chance of committing suicide than others? What symptoms do these kids exhibit? And is there any consistency among these so-called warning signs? The suicide questionnaire on the following page is designed to determine just who is at risk.

Psychological Factors. In a study of young people conducted in England and in Wales, researchers found that almost

SAMPLE SUICIDE QUESTIONNAIRE

INSTRUCTIONS:

Please circle the number that fits best. These questions pertain to just the past two weeks. The numbers you circle have the following meaning:

0 = Never
1 = Once
2 = 1–2 times a week
3 = 3–4 times a week
4 = daily

To evaluate the results, add up the point totals for each question. The higher your total score, the greater your risk of suicide.

How often have you:

1.	thought that you would be better off dead?	0	1	2	3	4
2.	dreamed about death?	0	1	2	3	4
3.	had ideas about killing yourself?	0	1	2	3	4
4.	thought that the world would be better off without you?	0	1	2	3	4
5.	thought about death and dying?	0	1	2	3	4
6.	smoked marijuana?	0	1	2	3	4
7.	been in high places and felt like jumping?	0	1	2	3	4
8.	thought about ways to kill yourself?	0	1	2	3	4
9.	taken drugs other than marijuana or prescription drugs?	0	1	2	3	4
10.	gotten so discouraged that you thought about ending your life?	0	1	2	3	4
11.	felt like running into traffic?	0	1	2	3	4
12.	had a plan of how you could kill yourself?	0	1	2	3	4
13.	wished you were dead?	0	1	2	3	4
14.	felt that life wasn't worth living?	0	1	2	3	4
15.	drunk alcoholic beverages?	0	1	2	3	4
16.	thought about killing yourself but did not try to do it?	0	1	2	3	4
17.	tried to kill yourself?	0	1	2	3	4
18.	dreamed about killing yourself?	0	1	2	3	4
19.	had a plan to kill yourself, started to do it, and then stopped at the last minute?	0	1	2	3	4
20.	smoked cigarettes?	0	1	2	3	4

eighty percent of the subjects suffered from some form of psychiatric illness.[2] Most of these kids were quite depressed, but they also exhibited antisocial behavior—truancy, stealing, lying, etc. So too, many of these kids abused drugs or alcohol. And many were almost obsessed with the idea of committing suicide.

Researchers concluded that youths who suffered from such symptoms, particularly those who were preoccupied with the idea of suicide, were far more likely to commit suicide at some point in the future than were those youths who had no symptoms of any kind. Similarly, other researchers have found that those who successfully commit suicide generally talk about what they intend to do.

Environmental Factors. Young people who encounter a lot of stress at home are at a greater risk for suicide than those youths who live in a relatively stress-free environment.

There are many reasons why some families live under more stress than others. Arguments about boyfriends or girlfriends or friends in general, problems with discipline or with parental authority, all of these "crises" result in greater levels of stress.

So, too, parents who are themselves depressed can cause problematic relationships with their children. In many of these cases, such behavior on the part of the parents amounts to psychological child abuse and the children feel neglected and withdraw from the world around them. These kids are more likely to commit suicide than kids who live in a nurturing environment. Children who have been sexually or physically abused are also at a higher risk for suicide.

Peer Pressure. Kids often imitate each other. When a teenager commits suicide, his or her friends are generally considered to be at risk themselves. I remember going to a high school to talk to a group of students after one of their classmates had shot and killed himself. The kids were devastated by the death of this young man. His classmates couldn't understand why he took his life. His close friends were especially distraught and felt angry, sad, guilty, and even betrayed. I spent the entire day trying to help them through their grief. The next weekend five students from that same high school had to be hospitalized, three for depression and two for suicide attempts.

Is Suicide Hereditary?

Let's ask some questions about the typical family of a depressed child. What is this family like? Are the child's parents also suffering from some form of depression? What of the child's brothers or sisters? What of uncles, aunts, even cousins? In most cases, depressed children have one or more relatives suffering from depression, or from some other form of mental illness. Depression runs in families. The same can be said for suicide.

In one study, researchers examined two groups of children who had been adopted at a very early age. The children in the first group (seventy-one in all) were suffering from depression while the children in the second group were not. The researchers tracked down the biological relatives of all the children in both groups and found eight times the amount of depression among the relatives of the depressed children as among the relatives of the healthy children. They also found the number of suicides to be fifteen times greater among the relatives of the depressed children.

What do studies like this mean? Simply this. If your mother is depressed, you have a good chance of becoming depressed at some point in the future. If both of your parents are depressed, your chances of becoming depressed in the future are even greater. And if there is a history of such depression in your family, then you and the members of your family run the risk of committing suicide.

Suicide is preventable as long as the people who contemplate it are treated for depression. If you are thinking about killing yourself, or have attempted to do so in the past, then you need to get psychiatric help immediately. The stakes are simply too high not to do so.

PART FOUR

If You Think You're Depressed, Get Help

— *11* —

State-of-the-Art Treatment

Depression is difficult to describe. You might say depression is just a feeling. You might say it's like living inside a dark cloud— no light, no hope. Then again, you might liken depression to a state of paralysis. You can't think. You can't even move. You feel like you simply can't go on with your life. These kinds of feelings are incomprehensible to those who have never suffered from depression, but to those of you who have, they are woven into the very fabric of your lives.

My task as your psychiatrist is to alter the composition of this fabric so that you can lead a relatively normal life. To do this, I follow a simple routine. I begin by conducting a series of tests, both mental and physical, in which I assess not only your condition, but the possible causes as well. This I call the workup. Armed with the information it provides, I can begin to help you.

The next step is to put you on a specific medication and see if your condition improves. If one medication doesn't work, then I will put you on another. In most cases, this is enough. Most patients respond to one form of medication or another, and it takes relatively little time to figure out what that needed medication is.

If you do not respond readily to treatment, and this happens in some cases, then I will broaden my approach to treating you. I'll take a closer look at your physical symptoms (perhaps there is an underlying physical disorder causing your depression), I'll re-evaluate your personal history, and I'll try any number of alternative treatment programs.

The last thing I'll focus on in your treatment is the question of relapse. Will you never again suffer from another bout of depression? Or will you suffer from depression again and again the rest of your life? This is not an easy question to answer. In the final analysis, the chances of whether you'll suffer from recurrent depression depend on both the kind of treatment you receive and how well you stick to your program. It also depends on your genetic makeup. In many patients, depression is chronic and needs ongoing treatment. Whatever the case, I will try to minimize the chances of your suffering a relapse.

How exactly will I do all this? And where will you fit in as far as the treatment of your depression goes? Let's take a closer look at some of the patients I've treated and define what I mean by state-of-the-art treatment. In doing so, you will gain a better understanding of what you can expect.

The First Step: The Workup

Many of my patients are visibly depressed. I can almost feel their pain the moment they walk in the door. The first thing I do is take down their psychiatric history. Before I can help them I need to know how long they've been suffering and what they've done, or tried to do, to ease the pain.

As part of the psychiatric history, I usually conduct a mental status exam. I want to see if my patients can think clearly. I want to assess their moods. Do they really look depressed? Are they suffering from anxiety? Do they have mood swings? Are they hearing voices?

Then I ask them about their family history. This is an important question to ask because depression tends to run in families. What about Mom? What about Dad? What about their grandparents, their uncles and aunts, their brothers, their sisters?

This whole process is a bit like panning for gold. I sift through a lot of extraneous sand in order to pocket a few real nuggets, which will help me develop a clear diagnostic picture. The information my patients provide can prove to be quite important.

"My uncle was an alcoholic."

"My sister spent six months in the state mental hospital."

"My father committed suicide."

"My mother couldn't get out of bed before noon to save her life."

In addition to the in-depth interview, my patients need a good physical exam (for the reasons we discussed in Chapter 2) and a good neurological exam as well. In some cases, I might examine the records of family physicians, counselors, and other psychiatrists and professionals. Often, additional laboratory studies are needed.

I realize this is a lot of information to work through, but every piece of it is part of a puzzle that needs to be put together if the treatment is to be successful.

What Ever Happened to Andrea?

Remember Andrea? Twenty-three. Newly married. She had absolutely no motivation, no energy, and found herself unable to concentrate on even the simplest of things. Her mind would just go blank. Her husband said things were so bad that Andrea couldn't even write out a grocery list. Andrea was clearly depressed. And each symptom in her depression had become a part of the fabric of her life. The question was: How could I change the composition of this fabric? What methods would I use? And how would I help Andrea regain her love of life? Or at least her ability to cope with life's problems?

If depression is both genetic and biochemical, then all I need do is order some lab tests to confirm my initial diagnosis. Once I know exactly what the problem is, then treatment is a cinch. Right? I only wish it were that easy.

In Andrea's case, lab tests were inconclusive. Both her physical examination and her blood work were normal, and though I reordered a complete blood chemistry analysis, I found nothing abnormal.

I could have ordered a dexamethasone suspension test (DST), or a thyroid-releasing hormone (TRH) test, but I didn't. In most cases, the results of these tests are of little diagnostic value. The DST comes back negative fifty percent of the time, and the TRH test is not all that reliable and very expensive. And no matter what the results, the medication I use to treat depression is pretty much the same.

Andrea wasn't taking any medication when she came to see me. If she had been, I might have taken her off all medication for two weeks in order to re-evaluate the depths of her depression. Another factor in Andrea's case was that her family had a history of depression and depression-related illnesses. Her mother had been severely depressed and had gone into treatment, and her uncle was an alcoholic.

I put Andrea on medication immediately. If I had been in a psychiatric unit of a medical center, I might have delayed her treatment until I could get some lab reports, but that wasn't the case here. I started Andrea on a very low dose of a drug called Doxepin—a tricyclic antidepressant—so that she could get used to it without experiencing many side effects. She did very well on the medication. (Many patients respond readily to tricyclic antidepressants, so I use them often.) I saw Andrea each week for six weeks, and during that time I gradually increased her dose. Again, she experienced few side effects.

The good news is that Andrea is no longer depressed. Last

time I spoke with her she told me that she and her husband were planning a two-week trip to Acapulco. She was doing most of the planning.

How Much Medication Is Enough?

In most instances, the higher the dosage, the more effective the drug. If 100 patients were put on 100 milligrams of a tricyclic antidepressant per day, only thirty of them would really do well, but if those same 100 patients were put on 200 milligrams a day, then sixty or seventy of them would do well.

Patients need 200 milligrams a day for at least four weeks, and preferably six, so that I can determine if the medication is effective. If Andrea had not shown signs of recovery, I would have increased her medication over the course of a few weeks, gradually increasing her dosages by increments of twenty-five milligrams. In addition to this, I would have ordered a blood level of the medication, an analysis that tells me if Andrea was actually taking the medication, if it was being absorbed properly, and if the medication was in the therapeutic range.

Unfortunately, many physicians are tempted to switch from one medication to another before they have properly assessed the therapeutic effects of the first drug. Such an assessment takes time because the drugs need time to prove their effectiveness. A patient needs to be on the right medication at the right dose for the right amount of time for it to be effective.

If at First You Don't Respond . . .

Many patients respond to tricyclic antidepressants, which is good news in itself, but just as good is the news that there are many alternatives for those who don't respond. If tricyclics don't work, I'll try another kind of drug, monoamine oxidase inhibitors. If those don't work, I'll try something else. The important thing here is to keep in mind that no two patients are exactly alike. What works for one may not work for another.

The tricky part is in figuring out why one patient responds

differently from the next. Why does one patient respond to one drug while another does not? Or why does one patient respond to a tricyclic in four weeks and it takes another eight? The answers to these questions are as varied as the patients.

DRUGS YOUR PSYCHIATRIST MIGHT PRESCRIBE

Generic Name	Trade Name	Starting Dose (mg/day)	Usual Adult Dose (mg/day)	Extreme Dose (mg/day)	Therapeutic Plasma levels (ng/ml)
Amitriptyline	Elavil	75	150–200	25–400	100–250
Amoxapine	Asendin	150	150–300	50–600	?
Bupropion	Wellbutron	200	200–300	100–450	?
Desipramine	Norpramin	75	100–200	25–300	150–300
Doxepin	Sinequan	75	75–150	25–300	100–250
Fluoxetine	Prozac	20	20–40	20–80	?
Imipramine	Tofranil	75	50–150	25–400	150–300
Maprotiline	Ludiomil	75	150–225	25–225	150–300
Nortryptyline Aventyl	Pamelor	50	50–150	20–200	50–150
Trazodone	Desyrel	50	150–400	50–600	?
Trimipramine	Surmontil	75	75–200	25–300	?

One patient might be suffering from some sort of physical illness in addition to depression. Another might be psychotic as well as depressed. Or alcoholic. It could be the medication does not reach what we call the therapeutic range in the blood. This means not enough medication gets into your bloodstream to do the job. Sometimes the liver breaks down the medication before it can take effect. In other instances, patients are taking too much medication. Some simply cannot tolerate the side effects caused by the drug they are taking. The following section lists the side effects of drugs commonly prescribed for depression.

What About Side Effects?

Tricyclic Antidepressants (TC's). Five to ten percent of the patients taking tricyclic antidepressants suffer from a number of side effects, of which the most common are dry mouth, constipation, sweating, and blurred vision.

Other side effects include food cravings, sexual dysfunction, hypoglycemia, hypotension, lightheadedness, dizziness, feeling faint, heart palpitations, insomnia, restlessness, fatigue, somnolence, confusion or delirium (in the elderly), and seizures (rare).

Monoamine Oxidase Inhibitors. MAOI's may cause side effects similar to those experienced by patients taking TC's. Hypotension (lowering of blood pressure) is the most common complaint, and this is especially serious for the elderly because they may become lightheaded and fall. Other side effects include dry mouth, urinary retention, constipation, sexual dysfunction, confusion, agitation, insomnia, and hypertension (rare).

Lithium. Lithium seldom produces serious side effects. The most common side effects include nausea, vomiting, diarrhea, and hand tremors. Other side effects include weakness, dizziness, agitation, drowsiness, slurred speech, blurred vision, headaches, sleep problems, anxiety, lightheadedness, confusion, and hypothyroidism.

Some patients taking lithium have developed kidney damage while others have developed diabetes insipidus, but such problems are extremely rare.

Successful Treatment

There are many reasons why you or any other patient may not respond to any one drug. But once a particular drug has proven ineffective, it is time to move on to the next medication. The truth is that very few patients do not respond to one form of treatment or another, and by ruling out what

TREATMENT PROGRAMS FOR DEPRESSION

If one drug helps a patient recover from depression, there is no need to try another drug. But what's to be done when patients do not respond to treatment? Move on to another drug. There are a number of different drugs a psychiatrist might begin with. The following flow-chart illustrates which drugs he or she might use if a patient doesn't respond to the first drug.

I. Start with tricyclic antidepressants (200 mgs. for 4–6 weeks)

    A. Small response or no response

        1. add lithium (300 mgs. twice a day for 4–6 weeks)

    B. Small response or no response

        1. discontinue lithium

        2. add one of the following for 4–6 weeks:

            – Prozac

            – Zoloft

            – Paxal

II. Start with Serotonin uptake inhibitors (Prozac, Zaloft, Poxal) for 4–6 weeks

    A. Small or no response

        1. add tricyclic antidepressants for 4–6 weeks

            – imipramine

            – desipramine

            – doxepin

III. Start with monoamine oxidase inhibitors (Nardil, Parnate) for 4–6 weeks

    A. Small or no response

        1. add lithium

    B. Small or no response

        1. go to higher dose of MAOI's (80–90 mgs) for 4–6 weeks

        2. discontinue lithium

    C. Small or no response

        1. add tricyclic antidepressant to MAOI's

If you don't respond to these medications, your psychiatrist may consider electric convulsive therapy as an alternative.

doesn't work, we can find out what does. Keep in mind that eighty to ninety percent of all patients suffering from depression (in its various forms) can be treated successfully if they are given the proper treatment. Chances are there is a treatment program that will work for you.

The Case of Mrs. Lane

Mrs. Lane was the wife of a prominent businessman. She spent most of her time volunteering for one thing or another, but she never stuck with any program long enough to be of any real help. She enjoyed eating at expensive restaurants, with or without her husband. Every three or four months the two of them would jet off to Rio or Madrid or some such place for a few weeks. When her husband died of cancer at age forty-seven, Mrs. Lane became clinically depressed. By the time she came to see me, she had been depressed for over a year.

I vividly remember our first session. Mrs. Lane was wearing a mink stole when she opened the door to my office, though it was ninety-five degrees outside. She looked tired, restless, but she did not move from the doorway until I asked her to come in. She then sat down on the couch, put her head on her knees, and began to cry.

Over the next few months I tried putting Mrs. Lane on a couple of different tricyclic antidepressants, but for one reason or another, they didn't work. I started her on doxepin, as I had with Andrea, but she complained of a dry mouth, blurred vision, and a dizzy feeling. "I feel like I'm about to fall off the edge of a cliff," she told me.

I next tried supplementing her medication with lithium, but that didn't work either. Four months of treatment and Mrs. Lane was little better than when she had first stepped into my office. "What's the use?" she asked me. "Nothing's going to make me feel better. So why bother?"

The truth was, we had only just begun.

I decided to try Mrs. Lane on one of the new generation

drugs, a drug called Prozac, in addition to the medication she was already taking. These new generation antidepressants have fewer side effects. In Mrs. Lane's case, the addition proved effective. She was no longer as depressed, she had more energy, and she felt better about her life in general.

Let me make one final point. It is hard to lose a husband, especially when you are as young as Mrs. Lane. It is harder still to recover from such a loss. In addition to medication, I found psychotherapy to be very helpful in treating Mrs. Lane (more about psychotherapy in Chapter 12). I also suggested she get involved with a home Bible study group through her church. The support she has found in this group has helped her a lot.

The New Generation Antidepressants

Psychiatrists are always on the lookout for new drugs that might be used in place of the standard antidepressants. Many such drugs have been developed over the years—Trazodone, Prozac, Amoxapine, and Bupropion, to name a few. Some of these drugs are available in the U.S. Others are available in Europe. Still others are being developed. These new generation antidepressants have fewer side effects, and yet they work just as well. In a number of double blind studies, some of these drugs were tested against imipramine and found to be quite effective. I use new generation antidepressants quite often, and I believe that they will be used by more and more psychiatrists as time goes on.

Let's Talk About Prozac

When Prozac first came out in 1981 it was hailed as a wonder drug. It was as effective as the tricyclic antidepressants and had fewer side effects. Two years after it was introduced some 650,000 prescriptions were written a month. Prozac was even the subject of a *Newsweek* article.

But the news about Prozac was not all good. There seemed to be a connection between violent behavior and Prozac use.

Rock star Del Shannon committed suicide while taking Prozac. Other depressed patients became suicidal while on Prozac. "60 Minutes" aired an interview with a woman who had not been suicidal until she started taking Prozac.

Much of the controversy surrounding this drug was taken out of context. Depressed patients become suicidal. They also become violent. It happens when patients are taking Prozac. It happens when patients are taking other medications. It happens when they are taking tricyclic antidepressants, lithium, mono-amine oxidase inhibitors. Do these medications cause suicidal thoughts? Do they cause violence? I don't think so.

The truth is that many more people suffering from untreated depression commit suicide than patients treated with medication. Prozac is effective, has few side effects, and many patients report that they not only feel like their old selves, but that they actually feel better. They say their outlook and even their self-image has changed.

What About Compliance?

Some patients do not respond to their medication because they do not take it as prescribed. Compliance means taking your medicine as your psychiatrist prescribes it. It means you need to stay on the correct dose of this medication for the proper length of time (anywhere from six to twelve weeks). Compliance is one of the most important factors in the recovery of any patient. Without compliance, recovery is next to impossible.

I remember one patient of mine, a man named Max, who simply refused to take his medicine. He told me that all he needed was a "jump start" in the morning, and then he'd be fine. Every morning he'd drink three cups of coffee. Every afternoon, six or seven diet sodas. Max didn't bother with any of the medication I prescribed. As a result, he continued to suffer.

There are many patients who, like Max, do not take their medication as prescribed. Some estimates put the number at twenty to forty percent of all patients receiving some form of medication as part of their treatment. Some patients are dissatisfied with their treatment, others are discouraged by the seeming lack of progress, and some do not like the side effects. Some dislike taking medication no matter what. And some just plain forget.

Whatever the reason, psychiatrists need to know why their patients do not take their medications if they hope to treat them successfully. After a couple of long talks with Max, I finally convinced him of the need to take his medication as prescribed. After several months he felt much better. He no longer needed six or seven diet sodas in the afternoon, and he gave up coffee altogether.

But What If I Don't Get Any Better?

If you do not respond to treatment, and let me repeat that this is somewhat rare, you suffer from what we call refractory depression, also known as treatment-resistant depression. The trouble is, too many psychiatrists give up on their patients long before they have exhausted all of the possibilities.

When I was teaching in medical school at the University of Louisville, I saw many such cases. Many psychiatrists in private practice referred supposedly incurable patients to the university because they knew we had greater resources, and therefore a greater chance of finding a treatment that would work.

If you are suffering from refractory depression, the chances are you have been depressed for quite some time. You have been given all kinds of medication. You may even have received ECT (electric convulsive therapy). But nothing has worked. You are tired of going from one drug to the next, from one psychiatrist to the next, but you are also tired of suffering from the pain of depression, and so you are quite willing to go through the seeming rigmarole of blood tests and laboratory studies, willing to try one more drug in the hope that it will work, willing to listen to yet another psychiatrist. Here is a procedure that should be followed for treatment of true treatment-resistant depression.

1. The patient should be treated as a "new referral." The psychiatrist should do the following: retake the history and mental status examination; repeat physical exam and laboratory tests; reassess the psychosocial scene.

2. To determine if the diagnosis of major depressive illness is correct, the psychiatrist should consider the following questions: Are there psychosocial facters that can be improved? Are there physical causes of depression (thyroid, cancer)? Is the patient on drugs that are likely to cause depression? Does the patient have an alcohol problem?

3. The psychiatrist should also consider the possibility that rapid cycling illness may require mood stabilization rather than antidepressants.

Leslie's Last Chance

From all outward appearances you would think that Leslie led a wonderful life. She had two kids in high school, and both were doing well. She lived with her husband of twenty years in a spacious house on the river. She lived what most of us would call "the good life." However, for five years Leslie battled a severe depression. Some days she felt so bad she couldn't even get out of bed. She had no energy whatsoever. Just washing the dinner dishes was a major effort. She tried to kill herself twice.

When Leslie first began to feel depressed, she went to her pastor. He tried to get her to work through her pain, but she was unable to do so. She then went to a counselor who, after a couple of sessions, suggested she go to her physician. From there she went to one psychiatrist after another, five in all, and always had the same result. No matter to whom she went, no matter what they did, she didn't feel any better. The last two psychiatrists she went to said she was suffering from treatment resistant depression.

By the time Leslie came to see me, she had been on a

dozen different medications at one time or another. "This is my last chance," she told me. "I'm so sick of being depressed, of being so useless. Maybe my family would be better off if they didn't have to bother with me. I'm no good to them at all now. Not the way I am."

I treated Leslie like I treat all my patients—the in-depth interview, the mental status exam, the physical exam, the lab studies, and then the treatment program. I started her on a very small dose of desipramine. As she grew used to this particular drug, I gave her larger doses. Leslie's condition improved slowly but steadily. She was sleeping better during the night, and she had more energy when she woke up in the morning. Yet she was still showing some signs of depression, so after three months of treatment, I added lithium to her program. The change in her state of being was tremendous. Leslie was no longer depressed. She didn't waste each day in bed. She didn't want to. She was full of energy, full of life. She was back to her old self.

Electric Convulsive Therapy

For Leslie, the right medication did the trick. But what if you can't find the right medication? What if there is no right medication for you? What if you still suffer from depression after you have exhausted the various drugs? If this is the case, and it is the case with some patients, then perhaps it's time you tried electric convulsive therapy (ECT), more commonly known as shock treatment.

Let me tell you about one patient of mine. Her name was Anna, and she was sixty-seven years old. She suffered from depression mixed with symptoms of a psychotic nature. She was quite paranoid and seemed convinced that her neighbors were plotting how to steal her collection of potted plants, which she kept on her back porch. She didn't bother much about matters of personal hygiene and often wore the same clothes for a week or more.

When Anna first came to see me, I put her on a tricyclic

antidepressant right away, but I soon found that she simply could not tolerate the side effects. Her blood pressure fell, she complained of feeling lightheaded, dizzy, and before the end of the first week she fell down while walking to the bathroom and bruised her hip. Of course I took her off the first tricyclic and put her on something else, but once again, Anna could not tolerate the side effects.

After several weeks, I became convinced that in Anna's case medication wasn't the answer, so I spoke with her family about using ECT. At first they were against the idea. They didn't want Anna hooked up to an electrical current. But after we talked for an hour or so, after they realized that Anna had few options left, they agreed to give ECT a try. They made the right choice.

Anna received ECT eight times in three weeks, and afterwards she was an altogether different person, a more alive person. She was no longer depressed. She was no longer paranoid about her neighbors stealing her plants. And she didn't wear the same outfit two days in a row. She was doing quite well.

Much has been written about ECT. Many people fear that it is dangerous and causes irreversible brain damage, even though there is no clinical evidence to support this notion. In the past, ECT has been misused, and this is perhaps the reason why so many people, like those in Anna's family, are still wary of it.

Psychotic Depression and ECT

There is a lot of data on patients suffering from major depression along with delusions. These patients are out of touch with reality. Some hear voices. Others see things. Many are paranoid. Tricyclic antidepressants are effective in treating thirty to forty percent of such patients. Antipsychotic medication is effective in treating as many as fifty percent. The combination of tricyclics and antipsychotics is effective in some seventy percent of the cases. And yet not all of these patients respond to drugs. So what can be done? In a recent study of psychotically depressed patients who did not respond to medication, ninety percent responded to ECT.[1]

The Risks

With any form of treatment, whether for something psychological or something physical, there are risks involved. If you undergo ECT you will probably experience some memory loss coinciding with the time of your treatment. You may not remember what happened while you were in the hospital. But the risks you face are very small, especially when compared with the risks you would face if you had open-heart surgery or lung surgery. Keep in mind, too, that in some instances, ECT is the only form of treatment that will help. I have found ECT to be a safe and effective way of treating depression, and I will continue to recommend it.

A Final Word on Refractory Depression

True refractory depression is quite rare. Most of what is diagnosed as refractory is the result of inadequate treatment. And when patients do not respond to any kind of medication, to any kind of treatment, other factors must be considered. Some might be suffering instead from an undetected physical illness, perhaps some kind of cancer. Some patients might be suffering from an eating disorder, either anorexia or bulimia. Some might be in the midst of a psychotic depression, a condition that is often missed, while others might be suffering from severe personality disorders. Still others might have drug or alcohol problems.

If your depression persists after you have tried every method of treatment, and if your psychiatrist can find no other possible cause, then you may be suffering from true refractory depression. But fortunately, very few people fall into this category.

Depression and Anxiety

Ellen was thirty-five. She came into my office with all of the signs of depression. She had problems sleeping. She'd lost weight. Her energy was down. She cried a lot. But there was something different about Ellen. She told me she could feel her heart pounding, that she was often short of breath, that she would become light-headed. She told me that she also felt anxious and nervous most of the time. Ellen was suffering from depression with anxiety.

I see people like Ellen quite often, and their problem poses a dilemma. Do I treat the anxiety or the depression? The answer is that it depends. If the depression is the most prominent feature, I use antidepressants. If the anxiety is overwhelming (in some cases it can develop into a full-blown panic attack), I use an anxiety medication like Xanax. This was the case with Ellen. I stated her on Xanax to control her feelings of anxiety. I also started her on imipramine, an antidepressant which is also helpful in treating the symptoms of anxiety. Over the next few weeks, Ellen's condition really improved. She was sleeping much better. Her depression had lifted. And she was no longer plagued by nervousness and anxiety.

Relapse in Depression

Now let's consider your chances of suffering from another bout of depression sometime in the future, and what to do if you suffer a relapse.

One of my patients, an older man I'll call Harry, became depressed every September and stayed that way until January. Every year he came into my office in late August, and I gave him enough medication to last him to the first week of the new year. When Harry first came to see me, he asked me how long his depression would last. I told him I did not know. When he asked me how long he would have to take his medication, I again had to tell him I did not know.

The questions Harry asked are good questions, and they are the questions I hear most often from new patients.

"Am I going to be depressed like this the rest of my life?"

"Will I have to take my medication forever?"

"How long will this depression last?"

These are very important questions. They are also quite difficult to answer. I do know, for instance, that depression is cyclic, meaning that those who suffer from depression do so intermittently. They may be depressed for four or five months, like Harry, and then they may feel just fine for the next few months. Some people get depressed every Christmas. Others get depressed during the winter.

Unfortunately, I cannot predict how long you will suffer from depression, or if and when you will suffer a relapse. I can quote statistics. As many as fifty percent of those patients who have recovered from a depression will have another episode, and seventy to eighty percent of those who suffer from two or more episodes will suffer from many more.

If you have been depressed at some time in your life, even if you were very young at the time, there is a good chance you will suffer from recurrent depression for the rest of your life. But there is much you can do to minimize a possible relapse.

Continuing Treatment

Many of my patients want to discontinue their treatment the moment they feel better. I can empathize with their desire. They are tired of taking their medication, tired of coping with all of the side effects, tired of seeing a psychiatrist. But they must stick with the program if they hope to get better and stay better.

In one university study, patients who had recovered from a depression were given placebos instead of the medication they had been taking. Although these patients did not know they were taking placebos, half of them went back into depression. (This percentage is quite high.)

I have found that patients who stay on their medication for an additional ten-to-twelve months after they have "recovered" have a much lower relapse rate, so I tell my own patients that if they want to recover from depression, they need to stay on their medication for a year.

The Pitt Study

The more we learn about recurrent depression, the better we will be able to help those who suffer a relapse. Consider a study that was conducted at the University of Pittsburgh.[2] For three years, the researchers at Pitt studied maintenance therapy in relation to 128 patients suffering from recurrent depression. The patients ranged in age from twenty-one to sixty-nine, and each had suffered from at least three episodes of depression during their lives. For these patients, then, depression was not a one-time thing; it had happened again and again.

When the study began, the patients were not depressed, though they had been depressed in the past. They were "between" depressive episodes. The researchers put the patients into five groups:

Group One—received medication only (imipramine)
Group Two—received medication and psychotherapy
Group Three—received psychotherapy only
Group Four—received psychotherapy and placebos
Group Five—received placebos only

By the end of the three-year study, the researchers learned that patients receiving medication (Groups One and Two) showed a relapse rate of only twenty percent, while patients receiving psychotherapy without medication (Groups Three and Four) showed a relapse of between sixty and seventy percent. Patients who received neither psychotherapy nor medication (Group Five) showed a relapse rate of ninety percent.

What the Pitt Study Tells Us

1. If you have had three bouts of depression during your life, then you stand a good chance of suffering from recurrent depression within a year, and an even better chance (over ninety percent) within three years.

2. If you receive psychotherapy but refuse medication, your chances of suffering a relapse will drop to some degree.

3. If you receive medication alone or medication with psychotherapy, your chances of suffering a relapse drop dramatically. Medication with psychotherapy prevents relapse during the first year of treatment more effectively than medication alone.

4. If you stay on therapeutic doses of medication for three years, your chances of suffering a relapse drop to twenty percent.

Summing Up

The Pitt study is valuable. It gives us a greater understanding of the nature of recurrent depression. It also gives us greater insight on how to properly treat this illness. There are two things to keep in mind. First and foremost, patients need to stay on their medication. Compliance is absolutely critical. Secondly, patients need to be involved in psychotherapy (more about this in the next chapter). No one needs to suffer from recurrent depression, for recurrent depression, like any other form of depression, is most certainly treatable.

— 12 —

The Role of Psychotherapy

What do you think of when you hear the word *psychotherapy*? If you're like most people, you think of some poor soul lying on a couch in a psychiatrist's office and talking about his or her childhood. You may have even been on such a couch yourself. Of course there is quite a bit more to psychotherapy than a couch and a bearded psychiatrist taking notes, but this image does point to the essence of what psychotherapy is, namely, the basic relationship between psychiatrist and patient.

I am a biological psychiatrist, which means I treat depression as a brain disease. I use medication to correct altered brain chemistry. But I also use psychotherapy, for it helps many patients. Treating depression is not like overhauling the engine on a car. It involves more than the genetics of our human makeup. Treating depression involves who we are and what has made us so, and this includes everything from our families to our experiences to our hopes and dreams.

Many of my Christian patients can't understand why bad things happen to them. They blame God. Some feel that they have committed an unpardonable sin or feel that they have lost their faith. They feel that their needs are not being met. Other patients don't know how to relate to their spouses, their parents, or their children. They try to find self-esteem in their social position or their possessions. Most of my patients seem unable to put their lives in order. That's where psychotherapy can be helpful.

When I was teaching at the University of Louisville, I treated six patients with psychotherapy for more than three years. I met with them every week, usually for an hour. Sometimes we talked about what was happening in their lives at the moment. Sometimes we talked about their childhood experiences. Most of these patients were the products of broken homes. They had been abused either emotionally, physically, or sexually. Did they need those sessions? Were they helpful? The answer is yes. Those sessions helped those six patients to grow and put their lives into perspective. I think all of my patients would benefit greatly from counseling sessions.

First Meetings

First meetings are critically important. I must make all new patients feel welcome. I must help them to feel relaxed, at ease. I must convince them that a trip to the psychiatrist's office is not a bad thing. This is not as easy as it sounds.

Many people have a hard time getting up the courage to come to a psychiatrist's office. For some, taking such a step is like admitting that they are crazy, that something is really wrong with them. For others, a psychiatrist is just another in a long line of people telling them what to do.

If I hope to do any good at all, I must be able to break through these misconceptions, and once I do, I have taken the first step in establishing a positive, productive relationship.

Breaking the Ice

The friends of some friends of mine brought their daughter to see me. Her name was Carol. She was fifteen, had long black hair, and wore faded blue jeans and a red turtleneck. Her parents told me that her personality had changed dramatically over the last few months, that she was depressed at times, violent at other times. Carol's parents also told me that Carol was having trouble sleeping. "At three in the morning she'll sit down in front of the TV and turn it on as loud as it'll go. It's gotten so that none of us can get any sleep."

I invited Carol to come into my office and sit down, which she did, but then almost immediately she launched into an angry and rather noisy condemnation of her parents, their attitudes, their behavior, even the way they dressed. By the time she was finished, she was crying.

It was somewhat obvious that Carol was depressed. I knew it. She probably knew it. Her folks knew it too. But that was not the time to prove how knowledgeable I was about depression. I could have talked about how important medication is, but if I did I was afraid I would turn Carol off. Mostly I just sat and listened. I tried not to judge her. I tried not to be shocked by what she said. I showed her that I was not like some of the other adults she knew, that I understood where she was coming from.

Carol was, like many teenagers, frustrated with the way adults treated her. She was angry at the world, and I understood her anger. I know how hard it is for young people to grow up these days. And by the end of the session, I got the feeling that Carol knew that I understood. She agreed to come back the following week for another session. This was a welcome sign. It meant that the ice was broken.

To Be a Good Listener

Although every new patient has a story to tell, very few are willing to tell me everything the first time around. Most of my patients need a little time before they are willing to "open up," and even then I do not always get the whole story. Establishing a good relationship with a patient almost always takes more than a single session, and very often takes three or four.

To be a good listener I must greet you as you walk in the

door, shake your hand, look you in the eye, and give you a warm hello. Good listening is not a casual affair.

I must listen carefully and intently to the story you tell. I must not, cannot let my mind wander, and so I must focus on your every word, your every intonation, and I must do so to the exclusion of all else because I need to hear what you *are* saying as well as what you are *not* saying.

I also need to get a feel for your emotional state. Are you unhappy? Are you angry? Or discontented? Why do you keep kicking my desk as you speak? Why do you keep looking at the clock?

Only by such active listening can I hope to encourage you to tell me your story. And only by such active listening can I let you know that your story is well worth listening to.

The Role of the Psychiatrist

In the 1940s, Dr. Carl Rogers suggested that the methods or techniques a psychiatrist used in treating a patient were not as important as the basic relationship between psychiatrist and patient.[1] This belief has always made sense to me. If I as a psychiatrist cannot develop a good relationship with you, how can I hope to help you?

Rogers was the first to provide clues as to how psychiatrists could develop good relationships with their patients. He said that psychiatrists first need to have an empathetic understanding of their patients. This means I need to be able to put myself in your shoes, to "feel" what you feel, to experience what you are going through.

Rogers also said that psychiatrists need to focus on what is good about their patients. This means I need to be able to see you in a positive light, value your humanity, and accept you for who you are.

Finally, Rogers believed that psychiatrists need to be open and honest with their patients. I need to be in touch with my own feelings as we relate to each other and I must treat these feelings as reliable and authentic. This means I need to tell you what I think and how I feel.

To Put Myself in Your Shoes

If I really want to be able to help you, I need to be able to put myself in your shoes. But to feel what you feel, to know what you know, to experience what you experience, is far from easy. And yet if I am able to do this, then I will gain a deeper and more meaningful understanding of who you are, and I will be that much more effective in treating your depression.

A tragedy struck one of my patients, a woman named Helen. Helen had a beautiful, teenage daughter, an only child. Her name was Jan. Jan was a good student all through high school. She was named Homecoming Queen her senior year. And she was active in her church youth group. After she graduated from high school she left to attend Vanderbilt University. There, too, she was a good student, and she had plans to become a teacher when she got her degree.

Two weeks before Jan was to begin her senior year she was killed while driving home from her summer job working as a youth counselor in her church. According to witnesses, she simply lost control of her car, which then careened off the highway and into the ditch. Investigators were never able to explain why she lost control. There was no evidence of alcohol, and no evidence of any mechanical failure. Jan's car simply went off the highway, and she was killed.

Two days after the accident, I went to visit Helen at her home. She sat there on the couch, silent, immobile, angry, upset. And then she turned to me and said, "Why did this happen? Why did God let this happen? Why?" Then she stopped speaking, stopped looking at me, and began to cry. I could feel the tears welling up in my own eyes. I could feel some of her pain. I thought about my own daughter and how I would have felt if I had lost her. The pain of Helen's loss stayed with me. Later that night I lay awake in bed and thought about Helen. I could not sleep, and so I prayed.

When I get "inside" one of my patients, like I got inside of Helen, I find I am able to listen to them with a more attuned ear, and they seem to know when I am listening from the inside because they open up all the more.

What does it mean to truly empathize with others? Above all else it means to struggle to know them as they know themselves. This kind of understanding is essential to the relationship between the psychiatrist and the patient.

How Not to Judge Others

If you've come to me for help, you want me to treat you with a compassion that mirrors the kind of compassion God has for all of us. You don't want yet another judge; you want someone you can trust, someone you can tell your story to. Now I may find myself appalled at what you tell me. I may actually be quite horrified by what you've done. But I must try not to judge you. The Gospel of Luke makes this quite clear. "Do not judge, and you will not be judged. Do not condemn, and you will not be condemned. Forgive, and you will be forgiven" (Luke 6:37).

This is not easy. I've heard some absolutely horrifying stories from patients over the years. One patient told me about the incestuous relationship he had with his daughter, how he had slept with her, not once, but repeatedly over the course of several years. I cannot imagine why anyone would do something like this, for it goes against everything that I hold sacred, and yet I have to deal with this man. I have to help him the best I can, for he still bears the marks of the Creator. He is still a person, still a human being, still a child of God's creation. But it is very hard for me to get beyond what he has done to his daughter.

When you tell me your story, I am determined to treat you with the same compassion Luke speaks of, but at times I struggle to do so. The truth is I sometimes have difficulty separating the great worth of a person as seen through God's eyes, from the shadow of sin, which follows us all. And yet, when I have this kind of difficulty, I look at myself, at my own sinful nature, my own unworthiness, and I see that I, too, have shadows. So I pray to God, and by his grace, I am able to get my thoughts and perceptions in order. I am able to accept my patients for who they are.

You Are Important

The most important thing I can get across to my patients, no matter what they've done, is that they are important. I think this goes for everyone. No matter who you go to for help, you want to feel important, you want to be taken seriously, you want to know that you will be treated with respect. If I do not show you that you are important, then there is very little chance you will share with me your whole story. As your psychiatrist then, I must prove myself to be open, honest, sincere, and dependable.

To be sincere means that I honestly have your well-being in mind. I want you to realize that I care about what you are going through, and to that extent I will try to support you in the things you want to do. I will help you realize that you are important, that what you say and do counts. But this doesn't mean that I am always supportive, for such unbridled encouragement would actually be dishonest.

The story of one of my patients illustrates what I mean. His name was Jeff. He was fifteen and a good-looking kid. He had red hair and blue eyes and wore a Dodger's baseball cap and black high-tops. Jeff was exceptionally smart, and he had attended the best public school in the city for two years before he dropped out. He had spent most of the past seven months in his room.

Jeff didn't say much of anything when he first came to see me, speaking only when spoken to. He was sullen and passive, and though he answered most of my questions, he did so in a direct, clipped manner. I told him that he needed to go back to school, and I later told his mother the same thing. I also told her that she needed to be quite firm with her son. Jeff was very good at manipulating his parents, especially his mother.

"If he doesn't go to school," I said, "take away his computer. If he still doesn't want to go to school, take away his phone and unplug his TV."

The simple reality was that Jeff needed to go to school in order to get along in this world. And he needed to be pushed, shoved, or he wouldn't even bother. I liked Jeff, but I couldn't tell him it was okay to waste his talents, his time, his life. To do that would have been utterly dishonest. So I told him what I thought and felt. He was not very happy with me, but that will change over time, because I think he understood that I cared for him, that I had his best interests at heart. I think he knew that I believed in him.

If you, like Jeff, decide to do something destructive, either to yourself or to others, I will talk with you about other ways of coping with your problems. And as a general rule, I will advise you not to make any major decisions while you are depressed, for the simple reason that when you are depressed, you do not see the world as it really is. You see the world with the eyes of the pessimist. You should not get divorced, quit school, quit your job, or plan any other major change in your life.

Lastly, I must show you that I am committed to you, and this is what I call being dependable. I will show up on time for every appointment, no exceptions. And I will give you my home phone number in case you need to reach me at some odd hour. I can't count the number of times I've been wakened in the middle of the night by someone who needed to talk with me. Some of my patients have never had a relationship with a dependable adult, with someone who would take the time to listen to their problems, with someone who would take them seriously. I try to be that person for them.

The Wall Between Psychiatrists and Their Patients

For years psychiatrists kept a certain degree of "professional distance" between themselves and their patients. You could almost say they erected a wall. Psychiatrists stayed on one side and patients stayed on the other side.

The reason for this wall was to limit the amount of personal involvement between psychiatrists and their patients—certainly a good idea. Unfortunately, this wall also limited the ability of psychiatrists to establish good, working relationships with their patients. It prevented open and honest communication.

The kind of communication I believe in is not limited to the exchange of bits of information. It is something that takes place on a deeper level, a spiritual level. Such communication, because it seems to break down the wall between psychiatrist and patient, is called transparency. It has caused a great deal of debate in psychiatric circles, and at the center of this debate is the fact that some Christian psychiatrists share their faith with their patients, a fact that has many of my colleagues up in arms.

I share my faith with my patients. Many of my patients are Christians, so I feel completely at ease talking about matters of faith. But I also know that in some cases such talk is not appropriate. Some of my patients are not Christians. They do not really want to know about my faith or about Christianity. They have come to me because they are anxious or depressed, and so I treat them accordingly. But if one of my patients wants to talk about Christianity, then we talk about it. If one of my patients asks me where I find meaning in my life, I tell them.

A Matter of Faith

His name was Ned. He was twenty-three and came from a good Christian home. He did very well in high school, made good grades, was editor of the yearbook, and was popular. He was also very active in his church. But when he went away to college he started hanging around with "the wrong crowd" and found himself getting into all sorts of trouble. He stayed out late every night, drinking and smoking pot. He began cutting classes. Eventually he dropped out of school, and though he tried to go back to school on several occasions, he was never able to stick with it.

When I saw Ned for the first time, he was living with his parents and not doing much of anything. Occasionally he'd pick up a temporary job doing yardwork for a local landscaper, but most of the time he just hung around his parents' house. He had all the symptoms of depression. He couldn't sleep. He had trouble eating and was losing weight. He had a negative attitude about himself, about his life, and about the church he had once belonged to. He had lost his faith in God.

I started Ned on medication. Slowly, he came out of his depression, and as he did, we began to talk. Ned wanted to talk about "the meaning of life."

"So what do you believe in?" he asked me.

"I believe in Jesus Christ," I said.

"Is that where you find meaning in your life?" he asked me. "Through Jesus?"

"Yes," I said.

Ned and I talked about many things over the course of the next two years. We talked about my own spiritual journey, about my own struggles, my own doubts. And by then we were also able to talk about the changes that had taken place in Ned's life. For one thing, he now had a job working as a sales clerk at a clothing store. He was seriously thinking about going back to college. And he had begun reading quite a bit, two or three books a week.

One day he walked into my office and said, "I've thought it over. And I'm recommitting my life to Christ."

He was grinning from ear to ear.

Ned returned to college. He studied hard and made very good grades. He still had doubts, still struggled from time to time, and he remained on medication, but he was a different young man. He was a changed young man. Was it important to talk with Ned about his faith? I'm sure it was. I don't think I violated any of my principles in talking with him. I don't think I was forcing my views on him. But I do think that by talking with Ned, he came to a better understanding of what he believed in and, perhaps more importantly, why he believed it.

Cognitive Therapy: "Thinking" Good

Depressed people think the world and everything in it is dark and threatening. Nothing is as it should be. Nothing works out right. Because this is how they perceive the world, they perceive themselves as being inadequate and worse.

"I can't do anything right."

"All of my relationships are bad."

"Nothing will ever work out for me."

"I'm not helping anybody. Why was I ever born?"

The problem here, at least as far as psychotherapy is concerned, is how to help depressed people feel better about who they are. One approach to this question, an approach called cognitive therapy, has to do with changing the way depressed people think about themselves. The basic premise of the cognitive therapist is that "bad" thinking accompanies "bad" feelings, and that "good" thinking accompanies "good" feelings. If you can somehow change the way you think about yourself, you can change the way you feel as well.

Let me tell you about a patient named Pat and how I helped her to think more positively about herself.

When I first met Pat, she had been depressed for quite some time. She had seen numerous counselors and a few psychiatrists. She had been on half a dozen different medications along the way, and nothing had helped. As she talked about her life, I could see that she did not think too highly of herself.

"When I was young," she told me, "I wanted to be a missionary, but my folks just laughed at me. I felt I wasn't good enough. I wasn't smart enough either. I just barely made it through college. My grades weren't all that good. I couldn't concentrate on the material. Everyone else was so smart. What did I think I was doing? After college it was more of the same. I started working as a sales rep for a computer software company, but I lasted only six months. I had five jobs over the course of the next three years. I just couldn't seem to hold on to one. I guess it would be different if I had someone to talk to, but my parents don't seem to care and I don't really have any friends."

As I listened to Pat I was almost overwhelmed by the negative image she had of herself. No wonder she was depressed. When she finished talking, I had her write down some of the things she had told me. While she was writing I asked her, one statement at a time, if the things she had said were really true. At first she was silent, and I think a little embarrassed, but then she admitted, reluctantly, that they weren't that true—she had done some things right. I then asked her if she would rewrite each statement with "the truth" in mind. She did, and then we talked some more.

Often we believe in many distortions about ourselves, but when we examine these distortions more closely, when we ask ourselves if they are really true, we can often see that they are not. Pat learned that her negative thoughts about herself were a distortion of the truth. She learned how to question such thoughts, to pay less attention to the lies her mind was telling her, to come to a closer understanding of who she really was. She also came out of her depression.

Psychotherapy and Spiritual Growth

As Christians, we are called upon to grow and develop. We are called upon to "test the Spirits" to see if they are of God. Not everything that runs through our brains is of God. Not every feeling is of God. We know from the Scriptures that the "heart is deceitful above all things" (Jeremiah 17:9), so it is vital that we test both what we feel and what we think.

How can we come to know the truth about who we are? How can we, like Pat, learn to distinguish the truth from a lie? To begin with, we need to measure ourselves against the Word of God, for it is through the truth of the Scriptures that we may come to know ourselves. Since the Holy Spirit teaches us through the Word of God, since the Holy Spirit helps us to understand and brings us into the truth, we have to develop a sensitivity to his leading.

Secondly, we need to share our thoughts and feelings with those in our Christian community. I know from my own experience that my Christian brothers and sisters will listen to what I have to say. They will help me see the distortions in my thoughts and feelings. They will support me, and they will pray for me. Through this process, I will learn to distinguish that which is true and that which is not.

Life is a process of spiritual growth. Sharing our experiences with one another helps all of us to grow. This sharing is the means by which we demonstrate our faith in Jesus Christ. It is also the essence of psychotherapy.

PART FIVE

From Depression to Spiritual Wholeness

— 13 —

Depression and Self-Esteem

Life is more than not being depressed. I know many people who have never been depressed, and yet they don't know what life is all about. They have the impression that the "meaning of life" is something you can buy, so they buy all sorts of expensive cars, fancy boats, and beautiful homes. Others think the answer is to be found in power and position. They are all wrong, and many are absolutely miserable because of their misconceptions.

Let me tell you about another patient of mine to show you what I mean. Her name was Francis. She was in her forties, and had recurrent bouts of depression for the better part of fifteen years. Though she wasn't suffering from any symptoms when she came to see me, she told me that she felt like she was heading for another depressive episode.

"I'm just sick of being known as Andrew's wife or John's mother," she said. "I want to do something, be someone. I want to get a job, anything. I just want to have a life."

What she said certainly made sense. She told me that she always wanted to be a counselor, so I suggested she go back to school. But I think there was something going on that ran deeper than being a counselor or a teacher or a psychiatrist. This woman wanted to gain some insight into who she was. She wanted to know herself better. She wanted to find a sense of her own identity.

A Distorted View of the World

Even though Francis was not depressed when I spoke with her, she, like many of my depressed patients, had a somewhat distorted, negative view of the world. She had low self-esteem. That she thought of herself as "Andrew's wife" or "John's mother" was but one example. Many of my patients are immobilized by how they think and feel about themselves. They see themselves as bad people, as horrible failures. They feel they can't do anything right. They feel they just don't measure up. Most of them hide their feelings pretty well, so not even their best friends suspect how troubled they are. And yet they are troubled. They see themselves as worthless.

A Doubting Thomas

Thomas was a young man of twenty-four. He had been out of high school for six years, but he was plagued by self-doubt, by feelings of worthlessness.

Thomas graduated in the top three percent of his high school class. He was popular, a pretty good athlete, and he went to church on a regular basis. He also went to Dartmouth College on an academic scholarship. His family was proud of his accomplishments, and rightly so. They expected more good things to follow. So did Thomas. Unfortunately, his college career didn't work out as expected. He did okay for the first couple of months, up until Thanksgiving, and then he got behind in his studies and missed some classes and tests. He barely made it through his first semester, and didn't make it through the next. He dropped out in March of his freshman year.

For the next few years Thomas drifted around the country, sometimes working, sometimes not. He was a waiter in

Philadelphia. He drove a truck for a firm out of Atlanta. He unloaded boxcars in Jacksonville. He also stopped going to church. He had a very low level of self-esteem. He thought of himself as a failure. He was unable to see the gifts that God had given him or to see that he was unique. He was unable to get a sense of his own personhood.

Thomas is now back on the right track. He responded well to medication and no longer suffers from depression. His views of both himself and the world are no longer as negative as they were. He's going back to college next year, though no longer on a scholarship. He told me that he's already socked away five thousand dollars toward his first year's expenses. He also told me that he's started going back to church. He told me, and he spoke with great conviction, that he couldn't think of anything more important, more vital to who he was, than establishing a good relationship with the Lord. I agreed wholeheartedly.

What Is Self-Esteem Anyway?

What do we mean by self-esteem? What does it mean to have a good self-image? A poor self-image? In a nutshell, self-esteem is what we think of ourselves. And yet there's more to the whole idea of self-esteem than just this simple definition. Many different things go into determining the ideas we have about ourselves.

Self-esteem has to do with our own history, with how we see our successes and failures. Self-esteem also has to do with how we see others relating to us. How do they see us? What do they think of us? We often see ourselves through the eyes of others. Sometimes these eyes are harsh, judgmental, demanding. Sometimes they are loving, accepting. And sometimes we mistake or distort what these "other" eyes see. My patients often see themselves through the prism of such distortion. Their minds lie to them. They begin to see themselves as no good, as failures, as bad. They begin to think they have never done anything worthwhile.

One good way to look at self-esteem is to visualize it on a continuum. At one end of this continuum is perfect self-esteem. Imagine for a moment that you are a person with this kind of self-image. You look at your life and see that you have achieved everything you ever wanted to achieve, at least for the present, that you enjoy good relationships with others, and that you live up to the highest expectations. (I have never actually experienced this kind of self-esteem myself, nor have I ever met anyone who has.)

Now imagine for a moment that you are at the other end of the continuum. You look at your life and you see that you have no gifts, no talents, that nothing you do seems to work out the way you thought it would, the way you had hoped, and that you are to blame for everything. (I have felt this way from time to time.)

I used to think that most of us had a pretty good self-image of ourselves. We didn't think we were absolutely perfect (which we aren't), but we didn't think we were absolutely worthless either. I used to think that most of us were somewhere between these two extremes. But after treating countless patients over the years, I have become convinced that many of us are on the low end of the continuum. Many of us suffer from feelings of low self-esteem, though we may be quite adept at keeping these inner feelings hidden from others. Whether we are Christian or not does not seem to make a difference.

Where does depression fit in? Four studies conducted independently, one in Australia and three in the United States, all came to the conclusion that there is a direct correlation between low self-esteem and depression. The depressed patients examined in these studies held rigidly to demands and had some rather negative expectations about what they would experience each day. They were overly concerned and anxious. They were also easily frustrated, so they tended to avoid problems. And they felt a great deal of helplessness.

I have seen the same thing in my own patients. Those who

suffer from depression see the world in a negative light. They are overwhelmed by the simplest of tasks. They see everything around them, including themselves, as having no value. Their lives are devoid of meaning and purpose. And yet in many cases, after these same patients are put on medication and therapy, their depressions lift. They feel better about themselves, better about the world around them. This kind of response makes a great deal of sense. It's not that the world has changed, for it hasn't. These patients feel differently about the world because they're not depressed, and so they see themselves in a different light.

Am I Worthy?

In the late 1960s, Stanley Coopersmith wrote a great book called *The Antecedents of Self-Esteem*, which pulled together the data coming out of almost a decade of research on the nature of self-esteem.[1] This research grew out of the widely held belief that self-esteem was associated with effective functioning and personal satisfaction. In other words, the more success you experienced, the better you felt about yourself. Thus, self-esteem had to do with creating and maintaining this kind of positive attitude toward yourself.

According to Coopersmith, many of the people who sought help from psychiatrists, psychologists, and other professionals stated that they saw themselves as inadequate, helpless, unworthy, inferior. These people had great difficulty both in giving their love to others and in accepting that others might love them.

What did these studies teach us about self-esteem? Coopersmith pointed out that people with low self-esteem were less capable of resisting the pressure to conform to the will of others than people with good self-esteem. (How true this is for the many adolescents who seem unable to stand up against peer pressure.) He also pointed out that highly creative people had high levels of self-esteem. These people were usually active within their social groups, and they expressed their feelings frequently and effectively.

Coopersmith also came up with a definition of self-esteem based on the findings of these studies. He wrote that self-esteem is "the evaluation which the individual makes and customarily maintains with regard to himself: it expresses an attitude of approval or disapproval, and indicates the extent to which the individual believed himself to be capable, significant, successful, and worthy."[2]

The whole idea of self-esteem, then, poses a single question. Am I worthy? This is a very good question, and how we answer it determines not only how we feel about ourselves, but how we look at the world around us.

Children and Self-Esteem

Some of the studies that Coopersmith discussed in his book focused on children with high self-esteem and on the families of these children. The researchers involved posed a number of very good questions. How can we help children develop high self-esteem? What are the parents of such children like? How were these children brought up?

The researchers found that the parents of children with high self-esteem accepted them without reservation. These parents defined and enforced limits as to what their children could and could not do, but they also allowed their children great freedom within these limits. By allowing such freedom, they encouraged greater individual expression, and thereby encouraged the development of a positive self-image.

The researchers noted that such parents used less drastic forms of punishment when disciplining their children while at the same time demanding a much greater degree of academic achievement than did the parents of children with a less positive self-image.

The conclusions to be drawn from these observations reflect what many of us have known all along. Parents who have definite values, who know what is and what is not proper behavior, and who are willing and able to present and enforce their beliefs, will raise children who see themselves in a positive light.

If we want our children to have high self-esteem, we must possess it ourselves. The importance of these observations cannot be underscored enough. Since patients suffering from depression and anxiety also suffer from low self-esteem, they may raise children with low self-esteem. This fact alone makes clear the importance of correctly treating these patients.

Our Identity in Christ

Many of my depressed patients see themselves as sinful, as deceitful, as estranged from God. They are not wrong, but they only see part of the truth about themselves. They do not see themselves in the light of God's love.

In God's eyes we are important. And though we may find this idea to be unbelievable, or even impossible, it is true. God does love us, and because of his love for us, he has involved himself in our lives. What we need to realize is that how we feel inside often determines how we see ourselves. If we feel depressed, then we will most likely see the world through the eyes of depression and sadness. The world will seem a bleak place, a cold and heartless place. And though there be some truth to this perception, it is a distorted truth.

Where do we usually find our identity? Our self-esteem? I see myself in a number of ways. I'm a physician, an American, a husband, a father, and a Christian, and being a member of these groups gives me some sense of who I am. Yet I would still be a person without these "identities."

Most of the groups I belong to, most of the things I identify with, only give me a superficial sense of myself. However, one thing I identify with that gives me a strong sense of my identity, a strong sense of my personhood, is being a Christian. I am first and foremost a Christian. I identify with Jesus. Through Christ I get a strong sense of who I am.

The Vine and the Branches

Jesus used the analogy of the vine and the branches to illustrate how we receive our identity:

> "I am the true vine, and my Father is the gardener. He cuts off every branch in me that bears no fruit, while every branch that does bear fruit he prunes so that it will be even more fruitful. You are already clean because of the word I have spoken to you. Remain in me, and I will remain in you. No branch can bear fruit by itself; it must remain in the vine. Neither can you bear fruit unless you remain in me. I am the vine; you are the branches. If a man remains in me and I in him, he will bear much fruit; apart from me you can do nothing. If anyone does not remain in me, he is like a branch that is thrown away and withers; such branches are picked up, thrown into the fire and burned. If you remain in me and my words remain in you, ask whatever you wish, and it will be given you. This is to my Father's glory, that you bear much fruit, showing yourselves to be my disciples." (John 15:1–8)

To be a Christian, then, I must continue to grow in him, as a branch grows on a vine. With this in mind, I can see the hatred within me, but I can also see myself as a thriving part of that vine. I can feel the anger inside me, but I can also feel the joy of being joined to him. I can sense the coldness of my own heart, but I can also sense the warmth of his sustaining love. And I can admit that I fail, that I have made mistakes from time to time. The painful truths about my life are made bearable by my union with this vine. In Christ I find my true identity, my sense of self-esteem, my sense of self. With this strong sense of identity and the resulting healthy self-esteem, I can do more than just overcome depression; I can become a fruitful member of God's family.

— 14 —

The Road to Radical Change

In Matthew 3 we read that John the Baptist went out into the wilderness and proclaimed the Word of the Lord. His message was simple: Repent.

What did John mean? He meant much more than just being sorry for something we've done wrong. To John, repentance meant a change of the mind, of the emotions, of the will, of the heart—a change of the self.

The Concept of Metanoia

The Greek word for the type of repentance John spoke about is *metanoia*, a word that means willfully going in a new direction. In English, the closest we come to this concept is in the word *metamorphose*. And yet this word is woefully inadequate when it comes to describing exactly what John meant.

When most of us think of the idea of metamorphosis we think of a physical change like that of a caterpillar becoming a butterfly. We are astounded by the physical nature of such a change. A caterpillar is far from a butterfly. Yet physical change, however dramatic, is not as dramatic or eternal as spiritual change.

The change John spoke about is not physical but spiritual. And so if we repent as John would have us repent, our minds must be transformed, our hearts must be changed, our wills, our emotions, our very self must be made new. This kind of radical transformation is what we were created for. And the day we involve ourselves in this process is the day we begin living.

The Power to Change

The first step in bringing this change about involves belief. We're called on to believe that Jesus is our Savior, and we ask him into our lives. This kind of belief is more than a mere intellectual assent; rather, this belief fills up our whole being. When we ask Christ into our lives, the Holy Spirit gives us the power to become a brand new person.

To experience metanoia, then, is to experience a complete, radical transformation of the person within. Jesus said, "I have come that they may have life, and have it to the full" (John 10:10). In Christ I can look at my own life from a completely different perspective. Instead of worrying about how I'm going to get ahead, what profession I might choose, or how I will plan for retirement, I wonder how I can become the person I was created to be. Because of this new perspective, I come to a fresh understanding of who I am.

To be born again in Jesus Christ is only the beginning. Sadly, many of us stop at the beginning. We are born, but we do not grow. We do not develop as Christians should because we are not involved in the process of change. We are supposed to grow, to develop, to change.

One of the saddest things I have ever experienced as a physician is seeing a child with some kind of physical or mental deformity. For many of these children there is little or no chance for real growth, little or no chance for them to live up to their full mental or physical potential. When I was in medical school I remember seeing a pair of twin boys. One was normal; the other was mentally retarded. The parents brought their retarded son to the hospital for help. Sadly, there was nothing anyone could do for him.

If we look inside ourselves, many of us will see a spiritual retardation, a failure to grow and develop as Christians. We do not have to be this way, for growth, though painful, is natural.

The Family of God

As Christians who have opened our hearts and lives to Jesus Christ, we soon find that we are not alone. We belong to a family of fellow believers.

What does it mean to belong to God's family? In Romans 8, Paul writes:

> Those who are led by the Spirit of God are sons of God. For you did not receive a spirit that makes you a slave again to fear, but you received the Spirit of sonship. And by him we cry, "Abba, Father." The Spirit himself testifies with our spirit that we are God's children. Now if we are children, then we are heirs—heirs of God and co-heirs with Christ, if indeed we share in his sufferings in order that we may also share in his glory. (Romans 8:14–17)

In God's family we find a place where we belong, a place where we can grow and develop, a safe place where we can take a hard, honest look at ourselves, a supportive place where we can discover our gifts, our talents, our potential, a place where we are so loved by those around us that they call us into accountability. Within this family of love and support and growth we find our identity.

We will, as we would within any family, experience pain and frustration, hope and fulfillment, but we will also experience the joy of becoming God's person, the person we were created to be.

The Early Church

The key to the process of becoming God's person is found in the account of the early church in Acts 2 and 4. These followers of Jesus experienced true fellowship in the family of God. They accepted the Scriptures as taught by the apostles. They made the Scriptures a part of their lives. They understood the value of knowledge and so they spent a great deal of time learning. They were involved with each other. When the disciples gathered, they came to share of themselves, and of their own experiences as messengers of Christ.

The disciples felt a deep sense of awe, of excitement, of wonder, of mystery, and they shared those feelings with one another. They witnessed the power and the joy of Christ through signs and miracles, and they spoke of these things among themselves and to others.

The disciples shared their needs and concerns with each other. A friend was sick, a brother destitute, so they helped each other. They took time to be with one another. They knew that mealtime was a time of intimacy, a time of joy, and so they ate together. They went to the temple every day to worship together, to pray together, to praise God. They understood what worship was all about. They knew that they were a part of God's creation, that they were dependent on him for life itself.

And in addition to all this, they went out into the world and shared with others the story of Christ, his life, his death, and his resurrection. They talked about how to become involved with Jesus.

The early disciples didn't have many resources, but they did possess a fellowship that was vibrant and alive. They gathered together in small, intimate groups. They shared their lives with each other. They were a part of the family of God.

This is the type of fellowship, of intimate community that I can identify with. Within such a sharing, loving group, real change can take place. I can become a different person, the person I was meant to be.

An Illustration of Christian Community

In the late sixties, I was part of a small Bible study group in my church in Gainesville, Florida. Each week we met in a different house. The host couple was responsible for teaching that week's lesson. After the lesson, we shared our thoughts and our lives with each other. After this, we prayed together.

Our group was very informal. There was no designated leader, and so we could talk about anything we wanted, pray for anything we felt important. All of us were Episcopalians.

One couple, John and Lisa, had been part of the Episcopal church for years. John had a Ph.D. in chemistry, and his wife, Lisa, was into the "praise the Lord" renewal movement. I don't think John really wanted to be in the group at first, but he went along with his wife and sat there and listened.

Another couple, Dave and Kathy, had only just moved to Gainesville. Dave was the project engineer in charge of the construction going on at the medical school. He was a hard hat, crew cut and all. His wife, Kathy, was a homemaker and a mom. They were both old-line Episcopalians.

The third couple, Michael and Julie, had been members of our church for quite some time. Though they had not grown up as Episcopalians, they were very much involved in church activities.

The fourth couple, Eddie and Linda, had also just moved into the area. Eddie seemed very interested in what was going on in our group. Linda was involved in the renewal movement in a small way.

My wife and I were the fifth couple, and neither of us had grown up in an Episcopalian church. I had been a Baptist, and my wife a Presbyterian.

I don't think you could have brought together a much more diverse group of people. I remember thinking that I would not have chosen any of those people for my friends, yet we were meeting one night a week to share our lives, thoughts, and feelings. The only time we missed any of those meetings was when we went away the following summer. When we came back, another couple had joined the group, Matt and Diane. These people didn't belong in our group either. They were strange. And yet there they were, talking, sharing, praying, just like the rest of us.

What a motley group we were! We had all come from different economic, social, and political backgrounds. But we had all been called by God, as brothers and sisters in Christ, to become a community, a family.

The Challenge of Coming Together

The first few times we met we just talked about things in general. Our conversation was superficial, polite, nice. No one took risks; no one was willing to speak honestly. Our lives were all in order. We loved our jobs. Our kids were perfect. We had no problems. As a group, we were what psychiatrist M. Scott Peck calls a "pseudo community." We wanted to avoid disagreements so we made believe that everything was fine.

In truth, our group was facing its first critical test. By keeping our true thoughts and feelings hidden, we were sabotaging any chance we had of developing a real sense of community. Our meetings were boring. They lacked vitality. What kept us together? I suspect that we were all firmly committed to the Scriptural idea of community. We all shared a deep need for the intimacy such a community would provide.

As time went on, we became more comfortable around each other. We got to know each other more intimately. As we grew closer together, we became more and more aware of our differences. On a number of occasions this awareness led to conflict. Linda, the woman who was into the charismatic movement, would say "God spoke to me and told me . . ." and she would proceed to tell us what God had told her.

Inevitably she was challenged by someone else in the group. Someone would say, "How do you know that? What if it's your own mind talking to you, pretending to be God?" She would get defensive and say, "Because I know, because I know, because I know," on and on like she was a broken record. Those of us who were more theologically oriented pointed out the flaws in her position. Sparks flew. Everyone got angry or tense. Here, too, our group faced another critical test.

Some of us wanted to change the way the rest of us thought so we would all be in harmony with each other, so that we would all be alike. Some of us just wanted to have the last word. At times such conflicts went on for two or three weeks before people settled down. Then maybe a week later, a new conflict would arise. All in all, however, I think such conflict was a necessary part of our development as a group. We were just feeling each other out. Was this group a safe place? Could we tolerate our differences? Could we tolerate our anger? Fortunately, we soon found out the answers to these questions.

The Need to Share

During this process of confrontation, one of us moved beyond the conflict and the differences and shared something really personal. And when one of us moved beyond this barrier, the rest of us soon followed. We began to listen closely, intently, when someone spoke up. We were honestly concerned. "My daughter's been hanging around with a bad crowd. I'm afraid she's going to get into some serious trouble and I don't know what to do about it." "Our marriage is just falling apart. My husband's angry all the time. I can't stand it anymore." "My job is so difficult. I feel so tense, so uptight, that sometimes I feel like I'm just going to explode."

These kind of statements had a profound impact on our group. We prayed together for those of us who were troubled. We offered our support so that they might find strength. Our sessions together became a time of healing, a time of spiritual restitution, and as time went on, we became more and more involved with each other's problems and each other's lives.

Not all of our sharing had to do with crisis situations. One week we might devote all of our attention to the needs of one couple. We would listen to what was troubling them, and then we would offer whatever support we could. The next week, someone else might be having a rough time. The week after that, everyone would be fine, and so we might talk about some of the good things that had happened to us. The week after that we might talk about how a particular passage from the Scriptures had affected our lives.

I remember one evening in particular. Dave and Kathy stated that they had been asked to teach a Sunday school class, only they were a little apprehensive because they had never led any kind of class before. The group was able to say to them, "You have the gifts you need to teach this class. You can do it. We believe in you." Dave and Kathy discovered something about themselves that evening. They discovered that they had some very special gifts, gifts they weren't even aware of, but which were apparent to the rest of us.

Discovering Fellowship

A sharing, Christian community is a place of discovery. Our group became such a place. We discovered that we possessed many special gifts which God had given us. We also discovered that to face the truth about ourselves was not as bad as we had expected. "John, you don't listen when your wife talks to you." "Julie, when you feel threatened you begin to cry and nobody can get through to you." "Eddie, you are so set in your ways that sometimes we can't even talk to you." Every week we discovered a tiny bit more about ourselves and about each other. We could allow others to see us as we really were without the fear of rejection. And we learned that in spite of our imperfections, we were still worthy of the love of those around us.

This kind of close communion with others helped me to come to terms with who I was. I could expose myself, show my vulnerability, and still be accepted. In spite of my fears, my doubts, my sense of inadequacy, I was considered a valuable member of the community. And through the community, I began to grow, change, and become who God created me to be.

The Act of Becoming

We talk a lot in our culture about self-esteem, identity, finding out who we are. We go to classes on assertiveness training. We worry about having "our needs met."

In an interview with *Rolling Stone* magazine, Bob Dylan was asked if he was happier than he once was. He replied, "Happiness is not even a concept with me. I struggle with becoming the person I was created to be." What a great statement.

As Christians we are "becomers." We grow into the people we were created to be. We change. We develop. And we go from being very comfortable to being very uncomfortable. We move from the old to the new. We leave a life of boredom to discover a life of excitement and abundance.

The question we need to ask ourselves is this: How many of us are really willing to change? How many of us accept the challenge of John the Baptist to repent? In many of my patients I see a reluctance to change, to look at things in a new light. They don't want to. Even if they know that changing their perspective will help them, they still don't want to do so. I see this reluctance in many couples who have troubled marriages. They don't want to change, to compromise, even if their marriage is falling apart.

In one way or another, we are all reluctant to change our ways. We all resist change, even when such change is necessary. The old ways are good enough, we say to ourselves. They make us feel comfortable and secure. And yet we won't grow as people if we stick to the old ways, if we stay the same, and we know this. We must change.

As a teenager, when I made Jesus Christ the Lord of my life, I chose to become involved in this process of change and growth. Since then, I have struggled with this choice. For the road to radical change is found in relationship to Jesus Christ, and in the fellowship of the community of believers. This is where I find life—life in abundance.

Epilogue:
Getting Help

If you are a Christian and suffer from depression and anxiety, you're not necessarily sinning or out of fellowship with the Lord. I wrote this book to let you know that depression is a disease. It is caused by something biological, something physical. It can be treated with medication.

The thing that has surprised me the most is not that so many Christians are depressed, but that so many keep this fact to themselves, as if they've committed some unpardonable sin. Many Christians are depressed. But let me stress that it's not their fault. They haven't lost out on salvation. They're not out of fellowship with God. I know some think they are, but in reality they are not. How do I know this? I see such people every day. They come in with the same symptoms. They can't sleep or eat. They feel sad. They have no energy. They have stopped having fun. More than likely, their parents suffered from depression or anxiety also.

However, by taking the proper medication, these patients can turn their lives around. Those who felt they were no longer Christians will have a change of mind when they come out of their depression. I have seen patient after patient experience this kind of change. Just because you are depressed or anxious doesn't mean that you have left the Lord. And this is important to understand. Some Christians sometimes have suicidal thoughts. When you are in the midst of a depression, you don't have control of such thoughts. This is also a part of depression, especially severe depression.

What you do have control over is whether or not you seek out treatment, and you should do so as soon as possible. We are beginning to understand that early treatment prevents a lot of later problems. We know, for example, that patients who suffer from anxiety and depression have more physical illnesses than those who don't. So the earlier you seek out professional help, the better your chances of recovery.

So You've Decided to Get Some Help

Once you've decided to get help, you have to decide where to go. There are a lot of counselors around: pastors, social workers, psychologists, and psychiatrists. When it comes to choosing someone to help you, there are many questions you need to ask.

Whom Do You Choose?

For depression and anxiety, I recommend a psychiatrist who is biologically oriented, one who knows how to diagnose and treat these illnesses with medication.

Where do you find psychiatrists like this? Many psychiatrists who teach at universities or medical centers tend to be more biologically oriented than psychiatrists in private practice, although this is changing. Most psychiatrists have had some experience prescribing medication to treat their patients, but most of the psychiatrists trained in the last ten or fifteen years have a better background in psychopharmacology.

What about other physicians, family practitioners, interns, or obstetricians? These professionals can prescribe medication for depression, but in most instances, they don't really know what they're doing.

Should the psychiatrist be a Christian? Recently, I had a call from a mother who wanted a "Christian" psychiatrist. There really isn't such a thing. Psychiatrists may be Christian, but there's no real field of Christian psychiatry. I think it is helpful if a psychiatrist is a Christian, but if I were suffering from depression, my first thought would be to find a psychiatrist who knew how to use medication. If he or she were a Christian, that would be great. We all need spiritual direction. Many of my patients also get help from Christian counselors. But the important thing is to think medication first, for without medication, depression can become severe, even fatal.

What about talk therapy? Is it helpful? Therapy is helpful. I find that many of my patients need it. I use psychotherapy with my patients and advise them to attend group or individual therapy sessions. All of us need spiritual direction in our lives, and to that end I recommend pastoral or Christian counseling. For me, a weekly sharing community has been helpful. We study the Scriptures, share our lives, and pray together. I try to get my patients involved in groups like this.

Where can I find more information about depression? Many good books have been written about depression. I have listed some of these books in the section entitled Recommended Reading. You may also try a bookstore or your local library.

Notes

Chapter 1: Am I Depressed?

1. Zung Depressive Evaluation Scale, by William W. K. Zung, *Archives of General Psychiatry* 12, no. 63 (January 1965).
2. Social Readjustment Rating Scale, by T. Holmes and R. Rahe, *Journal of Psychosomatic Research* 2 (1967): 214. Reprinted by permission of Pergamon Press Ltd., Oxford, England. All rights reserved.

Chapter 2: If It Isn't Depression, What Is It?

1. Mark S. Gold, *Good News About Depression* (New York: Bantam Books, 1986), 197.

Chapter 5: Depression: A Thousand Faces

1. Paul Wender, M.D. and Donald F. Klein, M.D., *Mind, Mood, and Medicine* (New York: Dutton, 1982).

Chapter 6: From Great Pain to Great Joy, and
         Everything in Between

1. D. Jablow Herschman and Julian Lieb, *The Key to Genius* (Buffalo, N.Y.: Prometheus Books, 1988), 101.
2. Ibid., 114.
3. David Paroissien, ed., *Selected Letters of Charles Dickens* (Boston: Twayne Pub., 1985), 78–79.
4. Egeland and Hostetler, "Affective Disorders Among the Amish 1976–1980," *American Journal of Psychiatry* 140 (1983): 56–61.

Chapter 8: Depression in Children

1. Myrna M. Weissman, et. al., "Maternal Affective Disorders, Illness and Stress: Risk for Children's Psychopathology," *American Journal of Psychiatry* 144 (July 1987): 7.

Chapter 10: From Grief to Suicide

1. Robert Hirschfield and Lucy Davidson, "Clinical Risk Factors For Suicide," *Psychiatric Annals* 18, no. 11 (November 1988).
2. Cynthia R. Pfeffer, "Risk Factors Associated with Youth Suicide: A Clinical Perspective," *Psychiatric Annals* 18, no. 11 (November 1988): 652–56.

Chapter 11: State-of-the-Art Treatment

1. "Electric Shock Treatment of Depression" (from an interview with Max Fink), *Psychiatric Annals* 17, no. 1 (January 1987).
2. David J. Kupfer, "Long-Term Treatment of Affective Disorders: Lessons for PD," *Journal of Clinical Psychiatry* (supplement) 51, no. 6 (June 1990).

Chapter 12: The Role of Psychotherapy

1. Carl Rogers, *On Becoming A Person: A Therapist's View of Psychotherapy* (Boston: Houghton Mifflin Co., 1961).

Chapter 13: Depression and Self-Esteem

1. Stanley Coopersmith, *The Antecedents of Self-Esteem* (San Francisco: W. H. Freeman & Co., 1981).
2. Ibid.

Recommended Reading

Burns, David L. *Feeling Good: The New Mood Therapy*. New York: William Morrow & Co., 1980.

Bonhoeffer, Dietrich. *The Cost of Discipleship*. New York: Macmillan, 1963.

_____. *Life Together*. San Francisco: HarperSanFrancisco, 1976.

_____. *Meditating on the Word*. Boston: Cowley Publications, 1986.

Crabb, Larry. *Inside Out*. Colorado Springs: NavPress, 1988.

Foster, Richard. *Celebration of Discipline*. San Francisco: Harper & Row, 1988.

Gold, Mark. *Good News About Panic, Anxiety and Phobias: Cures, Treatments and Solutions in the New Age of Biopsychiatry*. New York: Random House, 1989.

_____. *Good News About Depression: Cures and Treatments in the New Age of Psychiatry*. New York: Random House, 1986.

Kramer, Peter. *Listening to Prozac: A Psychiatrist Explores Mood-Altering Drugs and the New Meaning of the Self*. New York: Viking, 1993.

Larson, Bruce. *The Presence: The God Who Delivers and Guides*. San Francisco: Harper & Row, 1988.

Brother Lawrence. *Practice of the Presence of God*. Nashville: Nelson, 1982.

Miller, Keith. *The Becomers*. Waco, Tex.: Word, 1973.

Peterson, Eugene. *A Long Obedience in the Same Direction*. Downers Grove, Ill.: InterVarsity, 1980.

Rogers, Carl. *On Becoming a Person: A Therapist's View of Psychotherapy*. Boston: Houghton Mifflin Co., 1961.

Tournier, Paul. *The Strong and the Weak*. Westminster: John Knox, 1976.

Wender, Paul H. and Donald F. Klein. *Mind, Mood, and Medicine: A Guide to the New Biopsychiatry*. New York: Dutton, 1982.

Index